BASIC ENGLISH
Story 3

The **Basic English Series** consists of:

Poetry 1, 2 and 3
Story 1, 2 and 3
Drama 1, 2 and 3
Language 1, 2 and 3

BASIC ENGLISH SERIES

Story 3

John L. Foster

Macmillan Education

Selection and notes © John L. Foster 1987

© 1987 'The Cream of the Country', Ken Whitmore; 'Truth, Dare or Promise?', Marjorie Darke; 'The Rainbow Clock', Susan Gregory; 'Only a Kid', Mark Peters; 'Belfast Saturday', Jenni Russell; 'No Holier Than Thou', John Griffin; 'The Light in the Dark', Robert Morgan; 'The Darkness Out There', Penelope Lively; 'A Sunrise on the Veld', Doris Lessing; 'Watermelon Moon', Borden Deal

All rights reserved. No reproduction, copy or transmission of this publication may be made without written permission.

No paragraph of this publication may be reproduced, copied or transmitted save with written permission or in accordance with the provisions of the Copyright Act 1956 (as amended), or under the terms of any licence permitting limited copying issued by the Copyright Licensing Agency, 7 Ridgmount Street, London WC1E 7AE.

Any person who does any unauthorised act in relation to this publication may be liable to criminal prosecution and civil claims for damages.

First published 1987

Published by
MACMILLAN EDUCATION LTD
Houndmills, Basingstoke, Hampshire RG21 2XS
and London
Companies and representatives
throughout the world

Designed by Linda Reed

Illustrated by Ursula Sieger, Joyce Smith and David Dowland

Printed in Hong Kong

British Library Cataloguing in Publication Data
Story 3. — (Basic English series)
1. Short stories, English 2. English
fiction — 20th century
I. Foster, John L. (John Louis) II. Series
823'.01'08[FS]   PR1309.S5
ISBN 0–333–44622–4

Contents

	page
1: The cream of the country KEN WHITMORE	1
2: Truth, dare or promise? MARJORIE DARKE	11
3: The rainbow clock SUSAN GREGORY	28
4: Only a kid MARK PETERS	43
5: Belfast Saturday JENNI RUSSELL	48
6: No holier than thou JOHN GRIFFIN	54
7: The light in the dark ROBERT MORGAN	66
8: The darkness out there PENELOPE LIVELY	76
9: A sunrise on the veld DORIS LESSING	94
10: Watermelon moon BORDEN DEAL	107

Acknowledgements

The author and publishers wish to thank the following who have kindly given permission for the use of copyright material:

Campbell Thomson & McLaughlin Ltd on behalf of Robert Morgan for 'The Light in the Dark';

Jonathan Clowes Ltd on behalf of Doris Lessing for 'A Sunrise on the Veld' from *This Was the Old Chief's Country*. © 1951 Doris Lessing;

Heinemann Educational Books Ltd for 'No Holier Than Thou' from *The Fight and Other Stories* by John Griffin;

Michael Joseph Ltd for 'The Cream of the Country' by Ken Whitmore from *Dandelion Clocks*, eds. A. Bradley & K. Jamieson;

Penguin Books Ltd for 'Truth, Dare or Promise?' from *Messages* by Marjorie Darke, Kestrel Books, 1984, copyright © Marjorie Darke, 1976, 1979, 1981, 1984 and 'The Rainbow Clock' from *Martini-on-the Rocks* by Susan Gregory, Kestrel Books, 1984, copyright © Susan Gregory, 1984;

Mark Peters for 'Only a Kid' from *Win Some, Lose Some*, ed. Jo Goodman, Fontana;

Murray Pollinger on behalf of Penelope Lively for 'The Darkness Out There' from *You Can't Keep Out the Darkness*, ed. P. Woodford, The Bodley Head Ltd.

Every effort has been made to trace all the copyright holders but if any have been inadvertently overlooked the publishers will be pleased to make the necessary arrangement at the first opportunity.

1: The cream of the country

KEN WHITMORE

When I got back to school after lunch I was met down the driveway by this girl saying: 'Ooh! You've knocked one of Anthea's teeth out. You're going to be in awful trouble.'

I went on my way in fear and trembling. I was very frightened of Miss Marryat. She never really did anything to be frightened of but she was a very forbidding figure.

So I met Anthea in the porch and there she was with her mouth swollen and a bit of tooth chipped off and her eyes all puffed up from crying, and we were told that when school started we had to go into Miss Marryat's study.

It was a very big room at the front of the school with a big bay window out on to the school gardens. It had once been a very big gentleman's house and this must have been the drawing-room, I imagine. It had a big Adam chimney-piece and in front of this chimney-piece was an enormous desk, at least it seems enormous to me now.

And there was Miss Marryat behind it. She always wore her academic robes and she had grey hair, drawn back, and she was a very tall, thin, beaky woman, and her eyes looked as though they'd been put in with two sooty fingers, all black all round. She always looked very sad — there was a great sadness about her.

We both hung back from telling her what had happened but gradually it came out in penny numbers. We'd been fighting about my hat.

I was a day girl at St Agnes's and every day I went home for lunch. If I didn't get this bus, the twelve o'clock, I was late getting back. And I had this friend called Anthea — Anthea Hardy — and she knew I wanted to get this bus. So I went into the cloakroom to get ready, dashing for the bus. The school was on a hill and you could see the buses, standing in at the bottom of the hill, because that was the terminus, so if one was in you could see it, just the top of it from the cloakroom windows, and if the engine was going you could see it shaking, a big red bus.

And I was getting ready when Anthea grabbed my hat.

I couldn't go without my hat. We had to always go out on the streets properly dressed, which meant we always had to have our hats on, and not at a rakish angle or anything like that. It was a blue velour hat with a blue band striped with cream.

We had straw boaters in the summer with very, very big brims — what used to be called bacon slicers. I remember this rule about wearing hats, always. I remember my boater blowing in the road and a car running over it, and Miss Magarach, the maths mistress, coming along the street and picking it up out of the road and punching the crown back in, it was hanging out all over the place, and putting it back on my head and making me wear it.

But it was my blue velour hat that Anthea grabbed, because it was winter.

I tried to get it off her and I pleaded with her, but she wouldn't, she threw it over the rails where we kept our coats, to somebody on the other side. They caught it and threw it back and Anthea tormented me dreadfully with this hat. And there was this red bus juddering away down the hill and any second it would be going.

And so I bunched up my fist and I walloped her. I just saw the blood spurting out and I grabbed my hat and ran. I ran across the road to get this bus. It was one of those old type with the open side and a handrail going down, and it was moving out, and I swung myself up by the handrail and on to it.

Miss Marryat was very put out by what we'd done and so she ordered us to go down on our knees and pray for forgiveness there and then. It was very high church, St Agnes's — so high church we all knew the Magnificat backwards, bobbing and crossing, practically Catholic.

I'd only just escaped going to a convent. There were two schools, you see, at either end of the village. There was the blue one, which I went to, St Agnes's, which was known as the Bluebottles, and at the other end there was the convent, with an identical uniform, but in brown and yellow, and they were called the Wasps. The Wasps and the Bluebottles. Mount Carmel. I always used to think it was Mount Caramel, and that's why their uniforms were brown. I remember my parents asking me which one I wanted to go to. Isn't it crazy? Well, I mean, you obviously opt for the one with the prettiest uniform when you're only eleven, don't you? The blue was infinitely prettier and more stylish. We had a very nice dark blue fitted gymslip, with a flared skirt, and a deep cream blouse and a lovely bright blue tie with a diagonal cream stripe; and in the summer we wore blue gingham frocks and our socks were deep cream with blue bands at the top. Our winter coats were lovely hairy Harris tweeds with great belts around them, double-breasted and leather buttons. They were fantastically expensive and I don't know how my father managed it.

Anyhow, here was Miss Marryat with her deep-sunk Saint Bernard eyes telling us to get down on our knees, but I was in one of my sort of I-don't-believe-in-all-that-rubbish phases and all ready to stand on principle.

Anthea was rather soft and pretty and sycophantic. She would butter up to any of the teachers and she was buckling at the knees and ready to go down and pray — when I declared I wouldn't. I didn't see what I'd done I needed any forgiveness for. And so, seeing my resolution, Anthea decided to take a firm stand as well.

So we were let out and we were told we had to go back the next day at the same time. By then I'd established physical superiority over Anthea, so when we got outside I got her on the stairs and I said: 'I'll knock all the rest of your teeth out if you pray.'

We were hauled up every day for a week. You know how *you* were at that age — standing on principles? Well, we thought it was a fight between *us* and they had no right to interfere in it, let alone drag God into it. Between us we'd forgotten about it. We went pony riding at weekends. We were quite friends again, but we were still hauled up in order to pray.

Anyhow, the following Monday Miss Marryat took us separately and Anthea prayed for forgiveness straight away.

Then Miss Marryat called me in on my own. By now it had got to be a very big thing with me not to pray, I was picturing myself like Edith Cavell in front of the firing squad. But it had grown into a big thing for Miss Marryat, too.

'Isobel Compton,' she said, 'God doesn't like your defiance.' Her eyes had sunk even deeper and I had to lean forward to see if they were still there. 'He's had occasion to be cross with you before,' she said.

That was over my newspaper round. I used to do a paper delivery in the mornings, so I could keep my pony, Penny. I used to wear a particularly lurid pair of yellow sailcloth trousers, which were warm, and I would also on occasions wear my school blazer. I had a big canvas bag which said *News of the World* on the side.

Miss Marryat was an early riser and the boarders' hall was at the other end of the village, and she used to sweep down the main street in her academic robes just as I was sweeping past with my *News of the World* bag and school blazer and yellow pants.

And so she had me up about that. God didn't like the idea of a St Agnes's girl doing that, she said. I told her my mother thought it was a good thing for me to work — that I was going to have to work anyway. But they didn't go along with that principle at St Agnes's. Their young ladies *never* had to work for a living. In the end we compromised. I carried on my paper round, but not in my blazer.

I remember lots of nasty things about that school. My parents kept a little pottery and ironware shop and all it was was a little wooden shack and we opened the front down on chains and that was the counter, and then we pulled down a shade and set out all the wares, and we lived in a barge on the canal, this tatty old barge. My parents thought they were giving me this terrific education or whatever at St Agnes's. They thought they were doing their best for me. It was £50 a term, so it must have been £150 a year. And that was a lot of money then. They thought it was very good for me, so they went without a good deal and they lived in this barge and worked hard at their pot and pan business to send me to St Agnes's.

I remember a beastly horrible girl. I can see her now. I was walking down the drive, pushing my bike. I was on my way home. There was this beastly horrible girl with very thin fair hair. It was autumn and the leaves were very crisp and dry and they were rolling along on the ground, making crispy noises.

And this girl said: 'Hm! Isobel Compton,' to her party of cronies — in a voice that everybody could hear. She said: 'Look!' she said. 'She's so darty that even the leaves are blowing away from her.'

I could have wrung her neck. Beast. But I didn't do anything. The time I flew at Anthea over the hat was the only time I ever really got my paddy up. I was solid to look at and solid in every way. Sort of stoical. I looked it as well. It's there in all the photographs of me at that time. I had a pleasant round face and short mousey hair and a fringe, and in these photographs I always had a smile on my face.

Anyhow, here was Miss Marryat, sprinkling a pinch of bonemeal into a goldfish bowl by the window, peeping at me over her right shoulder and saying: 'God is losing his patience with you, Isobel Compton.'

I felt my heart palpitating and my fists bunching up ready to wallop her, but I controlled myself and stared past her at the lawns rolling downwards to the road. It was all surrounded by rhododendrons like a park.

'Isobel,' she said, 'don't you like it here?'

I'd never asked myself that question and for a moment I couldn't grasp what she meant. It was like asking, Don't you like it in England? Don't you like it on this planet? Some horrible things had happened to me at St Agnes's, one of them was happening to me now, but it was what I knew. It was warm and snug. I didn't feel like leaving there. I had friends. Oh, I also had enemies but I at least knew who they were.

I hated the thought of having to face new kinds of beastliness in a strange place. You might think St Agnes's was a frightful place but I'll tell you a strange thing — I liked the school. I loved it, oddly enough. And one thing it did give me — massive self-confidence. You could hardly help it. For five years you had it driven into you that you were the cream of the country's young ladies.

'Isobel? I said, don't you like it here?'

I lifted my head quite proudly and looked straight into the hollows where her eyes lay buried and I said: 'Yes, Miss Marryat, I do.'

I knew exactly what I had to do.

'Then if you wish to stay you must learn to conduct yourself like a civilised individual,' she said.

I think she'd forgotten about the cause of it all — the hat.

'Our girls are moulded and groomed to grow into the women who set a standard in our society,' she said. I don't think she actually said, 'As an example to the lower orders.'

So I went down on my knees and I prayed like fury and through my half-screwed eyes I could see Miss Marryat looking — with a sort of pious relish — at my mouth working away silently.

'Oh, God,' I prayed. 'Oh, God, punish this stubborn old woman. Let her teeth drop out and her head grow bald. Let her goldfish choke on their bonemeal. Let the Governors sack her for being drunk—' and a lot more in that style.

'And God forgive me,' I prayed, 'for taking this easy way out; but praying for forgiveness for the hat would have been more dishonest still, and it was all her fault, and you know it if you know anything at all, which I doubt — yes, which I doubt — so there it is.'

And I stood up and smoothed my skirt down and looked at her as primly as I could; and she came across and shook me by the hand.

'I always knew you had the true makings of a St Agnes's girl,' she said. 'And now we're starting to bring it out.'

Thinking it over

1 When you read a story, it triggers off different thoughts for different readers. What were you thinking of as you read this story? Did it remind you of any times when you have been in trouble? Did the story end in the way you expected it to end? Talk together about your reactions as you read the story and say how you felt at the end.

2 What impression did the story give of Miss Marryat? What mental picture did you form of her? Without referring back to the text, write down how you would describe her character and her appearance. Then, in groups, talk about what you have written. Go through the story and discuss how the author presents Miss Marryat. Talk about how, by describing certain details of her character and her appearance, he enables us to form a picture of her.

3 What impression does the story give you of St Agnes's School? Do you think you would like to have been a pupil there? Give your reasons.

4 What do you learn during the story about Isobel Compton's background and about what she was like at the age of eleven? Why do you think the author includes these details? Why doesn't he tell us more about Anthea and her background?

5 This story is about a clash of wills between an adult and a child. Talk about why Isobel decides to pray for forgiveness. What do you think you would have done in Isobel's position? Explain why.

6 When the outcome of a course of action is the opposite of what was intended we say that the situation is ironic or full of irony. What is ironic about the ending of this story?

7 Talk about the title of the story. Why do you think the author chose that title? Do you think it is a suitable title? Explain why. Suggest some alternative titles.

Role play

It's a matter of principle
A girl or boy, who has been sent to the headteacher and given a detention, explains to a friend why she/he is not going to do the detention, on the grounds that it is a matter of principle and she/he shouldn't have been given a detention. Before you begin, work out exactly why the girl or boy was sent to the headteacher and why she/he feels so strongly about it that she/he is prepared to face the consequences of refusing to do the detention.

What's it all about?
A scene set in a present-day school in which a headteacher interviews two children who have been sent to her because they were fighting, and asks: 'What's it all about?'

How the author tells the story

1 This story is told in the first person. Do you think it would have worked just as well if it had been told in the third person? Say why.

2 a) At what point did you realise that the 'I' in the story was another girl?

b) What did you then think about the author's standpoint in relation to the story? Do you think he takes it altogether seriously?

3 Stories such as this are often set in boarding schools. Work out how much of the circumstances you would have to change in order to describe a similar incident in a comprehensive school. Try writing such a story, set in that different context.

2: Truth, dare or promise?

MARJORIE DARKE

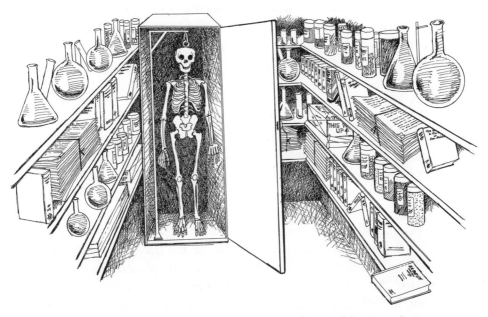

If it hadn't been a freezing cold day, Keith would never have joined in the stupid game. It was the dinner break and as he came out of the canteen a March wind like six freshly sharpened knives was blowing across the open grass, carving up his face and stiffening his fingers. It had stiffened his brains as well, he decided later, or he would have smelled trouble and kept away. But there was no idea of trouble in his head as he drifted aimlessly between the Science block and the gym to the playing field beyond, where he saw a bunch of his classmates dashing about — Sarah among them. It was Sarah more than anything or anyone else that kept him hanging about, although Froggie, Bill and Nige were charging around as well, and he was always hoping to be accepted as one of their particular mates.

The truth was he fancied Sarah. She went in and out in all the right places and laughed a lot and she never called him Titch like the others. Nobody knew he fancied her. At least he hoped nobody knew, though sometimes he had nasty misgivings about Puncher Webb with his meaty fists and squinty, knowing eyes. Puncher knew far too much for most kids' health. He made it his business to find out, and used all kinds of private information to make his victims squirm like maggots on fish-hooks. Keith knew all about the maggot treatment. Throughout the first and now into this second year at the Comprehensive, Puncher had made his life a misery. The nickname 'Titch' for a start, though that wasn't the only label. There was 'Duckie' because of his short legs, or sometimes 'Four-Eyes'. And it was Puncher's regular joke to nick his bag of crisps, gobble most and scatter the rest for the birds, or he'd drive him into some corner and shove stones or handfuls of grass down his neck. Once Keith had found himself flat on his back, Puncher kneeling on his arms and slowly dribbling saliva into his face. But worse than all these personal torments was seeing him pester Sarah — ruffling her hair, flicking spit-soggy paper pellets at her, nicking her gloves or her scarf and chucking them about. He was the worst kind of pain. To be carefully avoided if you hoped for a peaceful life.

But just as he was thinking these things, Sarah waved at him. Under his coat of icy skin Keith felt himself go hot. She'd never done that before. Never singled him out though she was always pleasant and friendly in an offhand way. He smiled weakly at her, wishing he was more like his brother. What would Alec do? Wave back or go and chat her up? Certainly he'd do something to get things moving, not just stand about dithering. Go on ... go on ... One foot was almost off the ground when Keith noticed two other separate happenings taking place at the same time — Puncher Webb belting after Froggie, and Hazel Goodrick watching himself watching Sarah.

Hazel called: 'Aren't you going to join in, Titch?' and sniggered.

Keith cooled off rapidly at the chilly notion that Hazel might spread it around that Titch Jameson was gone on Sarah Marks. She lived to gossip. Puncher would pelt after him cackling and chanting: 'Four-Eyes loves Sarah!' Everybody would laugh. Even Sarah might laugh. He couldn't stand that.

He turned away from Sarah, trying to look casual. 'Join in what?'

'Truth, dare or promise.' Hazel threw him a sly taunting glance. 'Bet you're too scared to play. Puncher's on.'

'I'm not afraid of him,' Keith lied.

'Come on then ... oh!' With a shriek she took off, whisking past Puncher's outstretched hand in the nick of time.

There wasn't time for Keith to opt out. Puncher, having missed Hazel, was bearing down on him, and Puncher wasn't going to listen to protests about not being in the game. *And* he was the size of a double-decker bus. Abandoning the urge to sock him in his fat mouth, Keith ran. He was a good runner, when there was space for it, but the gaps kept opening and closing at random as kids dodged and yelled and dodged again. He could almost feel Puncher's hot breath going down his neck, and in desperation made for the nearest gap only to find he hit a wall that was not a wall but Nige. They fell together on the rock-hard ground. Nige swore.

'Gotcha!' Puncher's ham fist closed on Keith's blazer and shook him. 'Choose then, Titch ... choose!' Another shake.

From the ground, Keith looked up through round spectacles at the grinning faces that closed in. Voices were urging him:

'Say then, Titch ...'
'Truth, dare or promise, Titch?'
'Which, Titch?'

He thought it was Hazel who said that. The silly rhyme set them falling about with laughter. Except for Sarah, but she was there looking at him, waiting to hear what he would say.

Puncher shook him again. 'Get a move on, Duckie Four-Eyes. What's it to be?'

'Get lost!' Keith tried hopelessly to free himself, but Puncher's bulldog clamp didn't slacken.

'Don't think I'll let you push off before you say. And you'd better hurry up or I'll shove your gob in that mud.'

He must choose where there was no choice. To say 'truth' would be weedy. The same went for 'promise', and Sarah was watching. He knew what Alec would say.

'Dare,' Keith said, trying not to imagine what horror Puncher would cook up. Around him there was a hushed expectant silence. He watched Puncher's narrow eyes get narrower and flick to the digital watch on his beefy wrist.

'Tomorrow ...' – he looked at his watch again, deliberately spinning out the instruction with cruel slowness – 'bring a plastic bag ... to school. It's gotta be ... big enough to hold ... a skull ... a *human* skull.'

There were whoops of glee and kids batted at each other. Hazel let out a screechy giggle. For one wild fearful moment, as he looked round the ring of grinning half-scared faces, Keith imagined it was to be his own skull deposited in the bag. But even while thinking it he knew this was stupid, and struggled to work it out. His brain was in a fog ...

Then suddenly he understood. There was only one skull in school that wasn't covered with live flesh and hair. It belonged to Henry, the skeleton that lived in the storeroom in the

Science block. Every now and again Henry would be wheeled out, bones rattling, for a Biology lesson.

The school buzzer blasted out a first warning to get ready for afternoon classes. Puncher began to gabble: 'Get yourself into the storeroom in Bio tomorrow. Open the skeleton cupboard. Take off Henry's head. Stick it in the bag. Stay put till the end of the lesson, then go down to the bog and stuff the skull in a washbasin.'

The scheme was workable, that was the cruel cunning of it. Keith knew that provided he could get into the storeroom without old Duffer Dawson spotting him, the rest would be relatively easy. And Duffer, who never seemed to see anything that was happening if it wasn't right under his nose, wouldn't be difficult to slip past unnoticed. Especially as he couldn't keep order for toffee and spent most lessons bellowing at kids to 'SHUT UP!' No, Duffer wasn't the problem, nor getting into the storeroom, though he didn't fancy hanging about in the half dark with a skeleton. In fact he didn't fancy any of it much.

'Knock it off, Puncher!' he tried to sound jokey, as if he didn't care. 'You're dropping me right in it. Duffer'll do his nut when he finds out. Imagine old Baines in Assembly. He'll be foaming.'

Puncher could and did, Keith could see by the slow, smug grin that spread across his ugly mug. 'So what! All you have to do is keep quiet. Nobody'll grass on you.'

But how could he be sure? Could he really trust them not to grass, even Hazel? And what if he got caught shoving the skull in the washbasin? These thoughts pursued him for the rest of the afternoon and most of the night, following him to school in the morning. The day seemed twice as long as usual, hours dragging towards the fateful Biology lesson last period of the afternoon. The only consolation was being noticed. All day, whenever they saw him, the kids in his year would nudge each other and come up to him, cackling, but somehow he always felt included. At break Froggie had offered him a piece of bubble-gum, and earlier, on his way in, Nige with Bill in tow had called to him: 'Hey, Titch, did you bring the bag?'

When he nodded Nige had let out a piercing whistle, and drawing level muttered: 'You really mean to nick old Henry's bonce?' with a snigger but also a hint of admiration that made him feel great.

'Course! Did you think I'd go back on a dare?' He was in it now up to the eyebrows.

Somehow he survived until the last period. By this time everybody in the class knew exactly what was to happen. They were keyed up even before Duffer arrived — fidgeting and hopping around in the corridor. The din was terrific. Before they had been in the classroom more than two seconds Duffer was roaring: 'SHUT UP!'

Nobody took much notice. The lesson, Keith realised with a sinking feeling in the pit of his stomach, promised to be the usual noisy romp which made it all the easier to do what he had to do. But he delayed as long as possible, although he seemed to feel eyes boring into him, watching to see if he would chicken out. Eventually he couldn't take any more. If Duffer copped him and sent him to old Baines it couldn't be worse than failing the dare. Puncher would dole out the maggot fish-hook treatment straight off.

Giving the plastic bag in his trouser pocket a last shove to make sure it wasn't visible, Keith eased away from his place, skirting round the end of the table and edging towards the storeroom door which opened directly off the classroom, next to the wall blackboard. He chose a moment when Duffer had his back turned and was bending over somebody's work.

The door to the storeroom was ajar, Keith discovered.

With a last rapid look back at Duffer, he pushed it just enough to allow his skinny body to tuck through the slot. Somebody cheered and he heard Duffer's voice boom out: 'SHUT UP! GET ON WITH YOUR WORK,' over the usual unresponsive racket.

There was a chill stuffiness to the air, as the storeroom had no window. The only light came through the partially open door. Two shadowy banks of shelving either side were cluttered with books, stoppered jars, beakers, cardboard boxes, kidney dishes, glass phials — none of which mattered. It was the sombre shape of the skeleton cupboard against the far wall which grabbed all Keith's attention. A problem that hadn't crossed his mind before walloped him now. Should he switch on the electric light or open the door wider and let in more light that way? He needed to see clearly because (and this was another unconsidered problem) he had only the vaguest notion how Henry was fixed together. After a few sweaty moments spent trying to make up his mind, he decided it would be less of a risk to quietly close the door and hope Duffer wouldn't notice than let sounds of himself and Henry wrestling and rattling escape, even though the pitch of classroom noise would act as a screen.

Closing the door and switching on the light was easy. So was opening the skeleton cupboard. Working out how to release the skull from the rest of the skeleton was another matter. He eased Henry out into the storeroom, twigging fairly quickly that he must unscrew the ring that protruded from the top of the skull and which hung Henry on to his supporting metal frame. The difficulty lay in preventing the headless skeleton collapsing in a heap of damaged bones while he, Keith, juggled with the skull. Really he needed another pair of hands. In the end he solved the problem by draping Henry's arms over his own shoulders while he unscrewed the ring. It was a curious sensation, hugging a skeleton. He expected the arm-bones to hang loose, and nearly dropped the lot when they seemed to stir of their own accord. A fizz of horror shot through his body. He was within a breath of giving in, but somehow hung on to his wits until he stopped shaking and could breathe well enough to carry on.

Doggedly he screwed back the ring on to the metal rod which stiffened the neck vertebrae. The relief of seeing the body-bones suspended once more on their frame was colossal. Before he had tackled this, he had lodged the skull for safety on a shelf, noticing that Henry had a full set of teeth except for one missing incisor. Now that he had finished rehooking the body, Keith took a closer look, wondering if the tooth had been lost in a fight or if a dentist had pulled it out. Weird how people's head-bones always seemed to be grinning when the skin wasn't there, he thought. Briefly the fizz of horror came back as he fancied that the grin broadened. Hastily he pulled out the plastic carrier-bag and shoved skull and grin inside. Then he settled down on the floor and began to chew over the thing that had been nagging him ever since Puncher's great mauler had closed on his shoulder the day before — how to turn the tables and get his own back.

He was not given much time to work out a plan. It seemed like less than five minutes (though it might have been longer — he hadn't a watch) when the door opened with a suddenness that made him jump. Puncher came in carrying a couple of enamel dishes.

'Everything okay?' He winked, smirking in a way that would have made Keith's blood boil if he hadn't been nearly crumbled by fright. The shock left him trembling. He glared furiously at Puncher, refusing to answer. Puncher seemed unmoved.

'You'd better get weaving.' He tapped his watch. 'Lesson's nearly finished,' winking again as if they were bound together by some comic practical joke. Keith thought he had never felt less like playing the fool than he did at this moment. He scowled, watching Puncher stow the dishes, refusing even a flicker of a smile in response to Puncher's broad grin as he went back into the classroom. It took another moment before Keith could handle the surge of resentment enough to start thinking positively again. When he did he realised he must act fast. The first glimmer of an idea had come to him; very foggy yet, and totally dependent on getting away from the rest of the class once school was over. They would want to hang around to see if he finished the dare. This was the real stumbling-block. Easy enough to slither back into the classroom with the bag. He checked over the storeroom. Henry's body was back in the cupboard; nothing else looked messy; he had the skull, right; but how to get away?

He was on his way back to his place at the table when Duffer, quite unknowingly, gave him his chance.

'Here, you . . . Jameson!'

Keith's heart did a double-take. 'Me, sir?'

'Yes, you. These forms need to get to the office before the end of school today. Take them across for me. The buzzer is about to go so don't bother to come back.' He held out an envelope. 'And the rest of you might get out on time if you'd sit down and shut up!'

Keith took the envelope, scooped up his books and shoved them into his satchel, then picked up the carrier-bag, nerves pricking, not daring to think how close he was to possible disaster. As he left the room a whispered gasp developed into a buzz of laughter and whistling. Duffer roared to no purpose. He didn't wait to hear more. Longing to sprint but making himself walk, he went down the stairs and across to the secretary's office in the Main block, willing the buzzer not to sound. It seemed the longest walk he had ever taken. After delivering the envelope he didn't bother to collect his anorak from the cloakroom, but made directly for the small path that ran alongside the Science block and away from the main gates and bike sheds. He didn't want to chance a meeting with Puncher, who was quite capable of sneaking out early to make sure of watching him. He couldn't cope with that. The light was dingy now and once or twice he thought someone was behind him making him turn quickly, but the path seemed empty except for moving shadows thrown by the row of windswept bushes.

The buzzer must have sounded by now, but it didn't matter. He had a head start. As he came out into the road the streetlamps switched on, but that didn't matter either. He knew the shops would still be open. The idea born in the storeroom was beginning to grow. Crossing over, he turned into the first of the jetties that ran between the old terraced houses, keeping to them until he finally emerged into a side street next to a butcher's, where Alec was sweeping the shop floor.

'Mind your feet!' The broom jabbed and Keith dodged, edging inside, glad that no one else was in the shop. 'And now you're here, you can take the steak Mum wanted,' Alec went on. 'Save me going straight home.'

This was an unforeseen hitch, but Keith hadn't much option but to do as he was asked. Not if he wanted Alec's help. 'OK.' He leaned against the counter trying to size up his brother's mood. 'Al, there's something I need for school . . . for Biology tomorrow.'

'Left it a bit late, haven't you?' Alec propped the broom in the corner and began slicing steak. 'What is it?'

Keith explained.

'Must be your lucky day.' Alec put the steak in a plastic bag, then went into the depths of the shop. 'Never used stuff like this when I was at school,' he said, coming back. 'What are they for?'

'Dissecting.' It was almost the truth. Keith opened the carrier and dropped the two plastic bags on top of Henry's skull. 'Thanks. See you!' He sprinted across to the newsagent's on the corner, reflecting as he came out again that it was just as well he had to go home first. It would stop Mum from having a nervous breakdown.

The kitchen was empty when he got in. Keith dumped the steak on the table and the carrier by his wellingtons.

From upstairs his mum called: 'That you, Keith?'

'Yes.' He went into the hall, not wanting her to come down in order to hear what he said. 'But I've got to go out again. A kid I know is going to lend me some homework notes I missed. Shan't be long.'

'Mind you aren't. Supper's nearly ready.'

Going back into the kitchen he picked up the carrier, hesitating uneasily on the doorstep before crossing to the gate. A few people were walking along the street. A car and two vans passed, followed by a cyclist. Keith shot to the other side of the road and took a short cut round the back of the scrap-metal yard, which brought him out into Robin Road where Puncher lived. Nobody had followed him, and yet he couldn't get rid of the feeling of being shadowed. Three times he spun round trying to catch a glimpse of whoever it was, but the way behind was always empty. He was almost glad when an old woman came out of a side road trundling a loaded shopping trolley towards him. She passed him without interest.

Puncher lived at the end where Blackbird Avenue joined Robin Road, and his corner garden was larger than those belonging to the otherwise identical houses — large enough for a vegetable plot and a shed. Reaching the Avenue, Keith checked on the old woman and saw her open her front door. As soon as she had gone inside he slipped in through Puncher's back gate, panting as if he had been in a race, hands shaking so much he almost dropped the carrier-bag. A street-lamp lit up the shed and shone in through its window. He sighed with relief, recognising the flashy frame of the bike inside. Puncher was home. At the back of the house a window glowed but the curtains were drawn. Telly sounds drifted out. There would never be a better moment.

Silently, keeping in the shadow of the fence, Keith went to the shed and tried the latch. The door opened. Inside he could just make out vague shapes of garden tools next to the bike, and what looked like a pile of newspapers in a corner. Under the window was a rough bench with a few flowerpots and an old washing-up basin. The perfection of the set-up hit him, and he began to shake again, this time with silent laughter. It took only a moment to make a newspaper pad to cushion Henry's skull inside the basin, but rather longer to fix the sheeps' eyes Alec had given him into the empty sockets. To do this he fashioned supporting cups at the back of the eyeballs with the Plasticine he had bought at the newsagent's. At one point, while working, the sensation of another presence was suddenly so real the muscles of his hands refused to go on moving. He jerked round. Empty shadow. Nothing else.

Keith blew out his cheeks and gave himself a silent pep talk. Nerves, that's all it was. The chance that Puncher might come in any minute for his bike. Wednesday was his karate night, and today was Wednesday. No good turning chicken when he was so near dropping that louse into the biggest muckheap of his life. No point in passing up the chance of watching the fun either.

He put the final touches to the Plasticine, then stood back to admire. They were a knockout! Light streaming in through the window, caught the slitty pupils and made them gleam almost as if they were ... alive? His shaky nerves wound to breaking point. He stared. They had moved. The eyes had twitched. Surely the reflected light had shivered?

Click click ... click ... click click click ...

Coming so swiftly after the shock of the sheeps' eyes, the small irregular dry sound drove him into panic. Forgetting to close shed door or gate, he catapulted out into the long Avenue, turning right and running half its length before realising he had come the wrong way. He paused, leaning against a fence, gasping for breath. There were people coming home from work now. One or two looked at him curiously. He forced himself to walk on, not daring to risk going back the way he had come. Hanging around Puncher's gate would be asking for trouble. There was nothing else to do but go home the long way round. At the last minute he'd gone and mucked everything up. What a raving nit!

By the next morning Keith's bitter disappointment had eased. After all, he had done the important part. Puncher was lumbered. Any last lingering regret vanished entirely when he got to school and found he was the centre of attention. In the cloakroom kids swarmed round him like flies. Sarah started the questions flowing.

'Did you do it?' She was gazing at him, eager to hear what *he* had to say!

'Yes, did you, Titch?'

'What happened?'

'Did anybody see?'

'I looked in the bog ... there wasn't no skull.'

'Go on, Titch, tell us what happened. Did you finish the dare?'

Through a space between two heads, Keith saw Puncher. Usually he would burst into the cloakroom, jabbering, whistling, swinging his bag, yelling. Today he was quiet, edging in as if he wanted to blend with the radiator or disappear behind the lockers.

'Ask him,' Keith said loudly, pointing. 'He knows, don't you, Puncher?'

All the eyes turned, but it was at Keith that Puncher looked for one brief instant before his gaze shifted and fell.

'About what?' he muttered, examining the floor.

'About the dare. Tell them what happened.' Keith was relentless, revelling in this unfamiliar sense of power. 'They all want to know if I finished it.'

Puncher went on studying the floor with care. 'He finished it. I ... saw.' Picking up his bag, he barged out.

There were a few groans. 'Is that all?' 'A dead loss!' 'What's got into him, then?'

'What are you grinning at, Titch?' Nige asked.

'Oh ... nothing,' Keith said. But it was everything. Titch Jameson, Duckie Four-Eyes, had fixed the Mighty Puncher. A life of peace stretched ahead. He took the first step into it as he left the cloakroom, heading across the courtyard to his houseroom.

Puncher was waiting for him a few yards from the swing-doors.

A lurch of the old fear came back. Then the new Keith remembered who was boss. 'Want something?'

'How did you do it? With only that one squitty bag ... I mean, how *did* you?'

Keith eyed him with suspicion. 'What are you talking about?'

'Me walking into the shed and finding the whole bloody skeleton sitting on my bike.' Puncher didn't mention the eyes, and Keith felt obscurely insulted by this ignoring of his masterpiece, even while frantically trying to catch fragments of his brain, which felt as if it had just exploded. Vivid memories of the night before jostled and pushed in no order. Sensations of being followed, watched, never alone, and the strange clicking rattle ... of bones? Had Henry walked with him all the way?

Puncher went on hoarsely: 'You mean stinking tick,

Bloody 'ell, you might tell me how you did it. How am I supposed to get that lot back before they're missed, Titch?'

'Keith,' Keith corrected, marshalling his wits. 'My name, remember.' He began to walk away. Paused. Turned. 'It's for you to work out — your bit of the dare. Call it a bonus.' He turned again and saw Sarah about to go into the house-room. She saw him and waited. Altogether a different sort of bonus, he thought — and went to join her.

Thinking it over

1 The previous story was about a conflict between an adult and a child; in this case the conflict is between two children. What is the relationship between Keith and Puncher at the beginning of the story? How and why has it changed by the end of the story?

2 Discuss the plot of the story and draw a diagram, chart or storyboard showing how it develops. Did the ending surprise you or did you pick up the clues the author drops at certain points in the latter part of the story? Use asterisks on your diagram/chart/storyboard to show where these clues occur.

3 Talk about what Keith is feeling at each point in the story. Choose words to describe his feelings and use arrows to indicate on your diagram/chart/storyboard what his feelings are at each point.

4 What part does Sarah play in the story? Do you think she will behave differently towards Keith in the future? Do you think Keith will tell her exactly what happened? How do you think she will react if he does?

5 What is your final impression of Puncher? Talk about how he is presented in the story. How much information are you given about his background and about why he is a bully? Do you think the story would have been more effective or less effective if the author had told you more about Puncher?

6 This story is set in a modern comprehensive school. Do you think it would have worked as well if it had been set in a different type of school, e.g. a boys' boarding school or in a different time, e.g. fifty or a hundred years ago? Give your reasons for your view.

Role play

How did you do it?
A scene in which one of the other pupils, who has heard that the whole skeleton is missing, asks Keith how he did it. Keith tells him exactly what he did and together they discuss the only possible explanation.

The dare
In groups, talk about any dares in which you have been involved. Develop a series of scenes centred on a dare.

How the author tells the story

1 Here is an example of the opposite point of view to the last story: a female writer thinking her way into the competitiveness between a couple of schoolboys. Why do you think authors choose to describe incidents that they can't have experienced completely themselves? Try it yourself. If you are a girl, write a story about the rivalry between two boys. If you are a boy, write a story about the rivalry between two girls.

2 a) There is a switch towards the end of the story, when what has been totally credible tips into the realms of fantasy. Did you mind? Did it make it a better or a worse story for you?

b) Try rewriting the ending with all of it being totally credible. Is it as effective? Does the final reference to Sarah still tie up the story conclusively?

3: The rainbow clock

SUSAN GREGORY

'Dear Delroy,' wrote Surinder. 'How are you? I hope you are doing well in school.'

Surinder stared in front of him at the objects on his desk top. His dad had bought him the desk only this year, so that he could study in his bedroom. That's what he ought to be doing, studying, not struggling with a letter to blooming Delroy. Surinder began to arrange his biros and pencils in a neat line along the desk top, and straightened every book and every piece of paper. Then he took the pencils out of the straight line and sharpened every one. With a sigh he returned at last to the letter. He read through what he had written five times, and stared in front of him again.

Surinder hated writing letters. He hated it at any time, but tonight there were so many other things he ought to be doing. There was his Biology homework for a start. Then he wanted to revise Chemistry for half an hour and work on some Physics problems for another half and then read the paper for fifteen minutes (so important to keep up with World Events). He looked in despair at the three pages of closely packed writing that his friend from Birmingham had sent and he sighed. Hadn't Delroy anything better to do these days? When they'd lived next door to one another before Surinder had moved to Leicester, they used to spend every evening together, studying. They'd done projects together. They'd tested one another when it came to exams. They'd built kits together when Surinder's timetable said 'Half an Hour's Necessary Relaxation Time'. Delroy had even copied Surinder's timetable, so that when it was 9.55 p.m., 'Time for a Relaxing Drink and Fifteen Minutes with Newspaper And/Or First Half of "News at Ten"', Surinder knew that next door Delroy would know it was time for exactly the same thing.

Now Delroy had time on his hands, it seemed, to squander writing a whole lot of rubbish about *girls*! Surinder snorted.

He got up and drew his bedroom curtains together so that they lined up exactly and sat down again and took up his pen. He was the only person he knew to use proper ink and a fountain pen, just like his father had before. He carefully drew a hair out of the nib and wiped his fingers on a tissue from the box he had covered with computer paper and labelled TISSUES in bold black ink. He was proud of that touch. 'Something a little bit *different*,' he had said to Delroy when he came to stay. Delroy had thought his room was great. Everything in it was black and white — black and white graph-paper curtains, a white Anglepoise lamp on his black fibreglass desk, filing cabinet white with black handles, black and white chess set cover on his bed, black and white digital clock on the white table by the bedside. Only the carpet was beige — white would have got filthy, black would have shown up the bits. Surinder hated bits. There were no unnecessary objects on Surinder's shiny surfaces, no pictures on his gleaming white walls. 'Wish my dad had the bread to let me kit out my room like this,' Delroy had said to Surinder, running his brown hands with their pale pink nails admiringly over the lacquered veneers, clean as an operating theatre. He eyed again the tissue box neatly backed with computer paper and labelled TISSUES in bold black ink.

But the fact that Delroy might even now also be drawing a white tissue from a tissue box wrapped in computer paper and labelled TISSUES in bold black ink was no comfort to Surinder. Delroy was a dead loss these days, a waste of precious time.

'I am sorry I couldn't write this letter earlier on, as I am revising for the Christmas exams.' Surinder stuck his tongue down his pen top and whistled dolefully, pulling at his turban. He'd never be done at this rate. One sentence every five minutes. Surinder thought again.

'Will you write me at the most once a month, not once a week, as it is more economical.' Surinder looked at his watch: 7.41. His timetable said, '7.55: *If time*, go downstairs for Reviving Cup of Coffee'. There was no way he could take fifteen minutes just getting down the stairs. Perhaps he could squeeze in fifteen minutes of *The Times* and catching up with World Events? Or fifteen minutes 'Exercising Time: A Healthy Mind in a Healthy Body'? No, he'd only have twelve minutes and forty-three seconds at it now. Surinder shuddered. That wouldn't do at all. But twelve minutes and thirty-odd seconds struggling to write to his friend!

'I always find it hard to write letters as I don't know what to say. If English was my best subject, not my worst, I would find it easy. As you know, my best subject is Physics, next is Chemistry.' Inspiration at last! 'Talking about writing, you remember that white fellow Robert Russell (Rusty) you met when you were here? His ambition is to be 'aerodynamic engineer' yet he doesn't do any homework. For instance, Afzal was away for a week and I borrowed him all my school books so he could catch up. It took him just one night to catch everything up. Some time ago Robert missed 3½ days off school and he still hasn't caught up with the average pupils despite me and Afzal borrowing him our books *many times*.'

Surinder, encouraged by this flood, thought again.

'You remember that fellow Salim I used to write you about? Well I do not hang around with Salim so much now as he is usually absent.

'With best wishes.
   Yours sincerely,
     Surinder Singh (Mr)
      146 Upton Street,
       Leicester,
        LE2 4PG
         Great Britain,
          United Kingdom,
           The Free World.'
'P.S. Tomorrow is our first EXAM.'

Surinder looked at his watch. He leapt up, folded the paper so that the two edges met precisely, slid it into the envelope, flicked with his tongue to the right, to the left, and stuck the letter down with a bang of the fist. He took the stairs two at a time and made it to the kettle just as the digital clock flickered to 7.55 . . .

It was a week later and Surinder was struggling with composition again. In his English lesson this time. The exams were over, and they were back to routine with double English. Bor-ing.

They'd just done Duncan being murdered by Macbeth. 'I want you to make up your own newspaper,' said Mr Melbourne. 'The main story will be the murder of Duncan. Splash headlines. King slain at Thane of Cawdor's castle. You know the kind of thing. Exclusive interview with Lady Macbeth. Report on the foulness of the night. Feature on local superstitions — horses eating one another. That sort of thing. Then anything you like to make it lively — puzzles, adverts, sports reports, cartoons, special interest stories. Just use your imagination.'

Surinder groaned. A whole double period to be filled with all that *writing*! 'Anything you like,' he said. 'Just use your imagination,' he said. Well, Surinder simply hadn't *got* an imagination. And that was that.

When the bell rang at the end of the first lesson, Surinder had written at the top of his large sheet of paper, 'The Scottish Times'. Underneath he had written, 'King Slain at Thane of Cawdor's Castle'. Underneath *that* he had written, 'The king was slain last night at the Thane of Cawdor's castle. There is an exclusive interview with Lady Macbeth on page two. The weather was fowl. The horses ate one another. Inside you will find puzzles, adverts, sports reports and special interest stories.'

After that he'd been pulling at his turban and getting ink on his tongue from sticking it down his pen top and making very discreet popping noises. Surinder looked around at what the other kids were doing. Afzal was staring out of the window. Very very occasionally he'd make a mark on a piece of paper. He was counting how many BMWs went past the school in a week. Afzal meant to own a BMW by the time he was thirty. If too many went past, though, he'd change it to a Lotus Élite.

David March was staring at the ceiling where a spider

promenaded round and round the rim of the light just above his desk. Every now and then the spider would burn its feet and spin a hasty web. But it always climbed up to the same light bowl again. Surinder sighed.

Wasn't *anybody* working properly? Surinder's eye fell on Topaz Smith. She had her head down and was scribbling frantically with a pale pink plastic ballpoint shaped to look like a quill pen. Every now and then her shoulders would heave up and down.

Topaz Smith was a weirdo. She was always in trouble for her multi-coloured patchwork jackets, her floating scarves and her dingle-dangle ear-rings. She had a spiky red fringe and a streaky pony-tail growing out of one ear and went on and on in Discussion. Topaz Smith did not know her place and Surinder couldn't stand her.

Topaz dashed down the quill pen and snatched up a pencil. (She did everything in fits and starts.) She examined the end of it with a grand gesture, flung her fingers against the spiked fringe and groaned. Then she tore across to the waste-paper basket where she was soon joking with Candy Atkinson. Sir let them talk while they worked if they wanted to, which Surinder thought a grave mistake.

Cautiously Surinder left his desk and bent over Topaz's paper to see what all the scribbling was about.

Topaz had called her newspaper 'The Daily Rain'. She had drawn a huge puddle in the top left-hand corner with a giant raindrop plopping into it. 'Read "The Daily Rain",' it said, 'for the best in Splash Headlines.' Surinder snorted. Trust it to be silly! The front page was dominated by a single word picked out in vivid tartan. 'MACDEATH!' it read. 'By your raving reporter Jock Strapp.' The report began: 'It was Macduff who first beheld the gherrizzly, gherrastly, gherrimish sight. "There was only one word for it," Macduff was quoted as saying, "MAC abre."' Surinder snorted again, quickly scanning the headlines of the other news items:

> HAGGIS WORKERS SAY 'NO' TO SOYA BEAN
> LEYLAND CARTS GO ON STRIKE
> STUPID BOY TO LIVE ON PIG FARM

And the advertisements:

> 'Bill's kilts: With sporran. Complete satisfaction guaranteed.
> Send large carrier pigeon to ...'
> 'Coffinmate. Coffee for Vampires.'
> 'Protect your sporran from MOTH.'
> 'Personal. Small dog requires large cat for *chasing round garden and* GENUINE FRIENDSHIP.'

Surinder looked at the Special Features. 'Exclusive interview with Society Hostess, Lady "Chi Chi" Macbeth. Page Three.' Surinder turned over the page. A cut-out picture of Joan Collins, showing a lot of cleavage and raising a Martini glass, winked up at him. Surinder closed his eyes. When he opened them again his attention was caught by something in the Sports Report.

> SEMI-FINAL OF SPLENDID MACJOUST
> Sir Hamish versus Sir Beamish.
> Sir Angus versus Surinder.
> Favourite to Win: Surinder Singer Sewing Machine. Six to Four On.

Surinder's mouth twitched at the same time as his eyebrows knitted. For his name was entirely surrounded with hearts! He turned over the page and caught his breath again.

For there was a huge picture of a very large turban, a maroon turban, *his* turban, upside down with a load of rubbish spewing out of it. And across it, so there could be no doubt, Topaz had scrawled 'TUR-BIN'. Underneath she had written, 'Top Quality Refuse Depository: SURIN'S TUR-BINS'. In spite of the insult, though, the SURIN was still surrounded by hearts!

At that moment Topaz bounded back. Surinder quickly flapped the page over.

'What you doing round my desk, Surinder?' demanded Topaz. There was a hopeful look in her eyes.

Surinder was caught off his guard. He couldn't tackle her there and then about the dread insult she'd paid him. Besides, he recalled Surinder, Favourite to Win, and the hearts, and he didn't know quite what to think!

'I ... I wondered if I could look at your Macbeth book,' Surinder said feebly, 'to get some ideas.' Topaz had her own copy of the play, new out. Her mum had brought it back for her, a present from London. Sir had shown them all. It was the real play but all done in cartoons. Sir thought it was great, Surinder that it was daft.

'Forgot it today,' said Topaz, crossing her fingers and edging her bag out of sight with her toe. 'But you can come round my house after school and borrow it, Surinder. Stay to tea if you like.'

Surinder could not believe his ears. Go to a *girl's* house? She had to be out of her mind. 'S'all right,' he said. 'Got too much work to do. Haven't the time.'

'I'll bring it round your house after tea then,' said Topaz straight off, looking at him with the bright eyes of a spider who has just netted a particularly dense fly. With a heavy heart Surinder settled back down to attempt another headline story. 'HAGGIS WORKERS SAY "NO" TO SOYA BEAN ...'

So quarter to four witnessed the unlikely sight of Surinder

Singh walking home with Topaz Smith. 'Can't stop,' muttered Surinder, eyes dodging this way and that. 'Haven't the time. I'll just pick the book up, then go.'

Topaz looked at him. She scrabbled in her peacock-tail-shaped shoulder bag and drew out a cartoon she'd done. It showed an alarm clock with a long grey beard, wearing a crown and a kilt, with a dagger up its nose and sitting in a puddle of blood. Underneath it said, 'Macbeth hath murdered Time.' She handed it to him. 'There you are, Surinder,' she said. 'Time's dead. You needn't worry about Time any longer.' Surinder looked at it and looked at her. He was at a complete loss. 'It's *sleep*,' he said scornfully at last. 'Macbeth hath murdered *sleep*.' Topaz stared at him. Then with a shake of her head and a heave of her shoulders she pulled out her plastic quill, took the cartoon from him, stopped at a wall, leant the paper on it and drew the alarm clock, some closed eyes and a lot of trailing ZZZZZZZZZZZZZZZs coming out of his bloody nose, and changed *Time* to *Sleep*. She put the pen and the cartoon away and bounded very close to Surinder. 'You're a slave to your brain, you know that, Sewing Machine?' she said affectionately, jogging up against his elbow. 'And *nearly* as boring as Afzal.'

Topaz stopped by the front gate of a terraced house in Norland Street. To say it was a terraced house doesn't make it sound very exciting. Surinder lived in a terraced house very similar to this one. That is to say, the same structure, the same stone scrolls on either side of the door, the same mangy-looking privet hedge round the tiny paved front garden. But whereas Surinder's house was a discreet fume-blackened stone with discreet smut-ingrained stone scrolls, and discreetly painted with the dark green paint that had become regulation for that block, Topaz's house was more like a child's idea of a house, entirely constructed of sweets. The front door was barley-sugar gold; the left-hand down-stairs window frames were a lollipop red and the right a peppermint green, while upstairs they were sherbet lemon and blackcurrant purple; the entire facing wall was painted milk chocolate, with one scroll the jewel colours of wine-gums, and the other, sugar-almond shades — soft pink, peach and the palest of aquamarines. Topaz's house looked good enough to eat.

Except you didn't eat houses. Houses, like schools, meant good solid achievement, the sound investment of time. Surinder sniffed.

Topaz opened the door. It wasn't locked. Instead of going into a dark narrow hall with the stairs leading steeply out, you stepped into a big room with the stairs going out of one corner. The Smiths had knocked down a wall. You could tell they had knocked it down because they had left bits of it lying untidily about.

The room was like a puppet theatre hit by the blitz. The walls that still stood were painted a fiery orange, the wall up the stairs was purple and the floorboards were red — no carpet, except on the walls. At least Surinder had the impression that the walls were a fiery orange or a deep purple but it was difficult to tell because everything was so sprinkled over with *things*. Suns and moons and planets and parrots and seagulls and pierrots-on-stars and babies-on-clouds dangled and spun before the eyes all around the stairs area, and in the main room were shawls and feathers and velvet and net and a black lace fan half-closed like a butterfly's wings, cables of sequins and beads, and posters and hanging plants and plaited string and jangling shells and bells. A moose's head with a sparkly necklace round it jutted out of the wall and the room smelt of moth-balls and wood smoke, marmalade, cinnamon and pine. In the middle of the floor was a grand piano. It was painted green where it wasn't all over flowers and ferns and fabulous beasts. There was no other furniture — just large cushions — and a great many books. No bookcases. They simply spilt and toppled about.

Topaz told Surinder to sit down and clattered off up the stairs screeching 'Mum!' The kitchen door opened and a little girl came out.

She looked like a child from a nursery rhyme with her blonde hair cut square round her cheeks and her full deep fringe. She was dressed in an all-in-one striped suit like a clown's with big red pom-poms down the front. She came over to Surinder and stood in front of him, staring. At last she said, 'Why you got a tea-cosy on your head?'

She didn't wait for a reply. 'I'm making up songs about carrots this week,' she told him. 'Do you want "Carrots Go on a Picnic" or "Carrots Cleaning Their Teeth"?'

Surinder opened his mouth. There was a colossal stampeding on the stairs and Topaz's legs appeared, followed by the bottom half of what turned out to be a large woman in a dragon-covered dressing-gown with a bandage of plaited scarves around her head.

'Surinder!' she said, holding out her hand. 'Hullo there. You've met William, I see. Take Surinder into the kitchen, Topaz, and let him find himself something to eat.'

Surinder was so astonished to discover the clown suit housed a *boy* that he'd followed Topaz into the kitchen before he'd had a chance to mumble that he hadn't the time. Surinder was glad he'd been told beforehand that the room he'd just entered was the kitchen because everything was dressed up to look like something else. The cooker looked like the Space Control Center at Houston, the table was a toadstool, the stools were mushrooms, and rose-coloured clouds floated past the window across a clear blue sky, though Surinder distinctly remembered it had started to rain. Topaz flung open a fridge door that had been painted all over with spiders complete with their webs.

'What would you like?' she asked, and Surinder peered in. He swallowed and thought desperately, deciding they couldn't interfere too much with a bottle of milk. What price a tissue box covered with computer paper and labelled TISSUES in bold black ink after *this*?

'Just a glass of milk, please,' said Surinder weakly. Topaz pulled a face but she handed him the bottle and a ruby red plastic drinking mug with a yellow plastic straw snaking out of it. He noticed she poured milk for herself in an *ordinary* glass, but to this she immediately added a dash of blackcurrant juice and stirred it all up with a spoon disguised as a spanner. She carved herself bread from a hefty-looking loaf and piled on a lot of purply pink salami. She held it up against the contents of the glass and nodded. 'I do so like my food to *tone*,' she explained to a mystified Surinder, taking a gulp of the violet-coloured milk.

As Topaz gulped, a multi-hued bird with wings like a feather boa flung itself out of a clock with a Kermit the Frog face and an upside-down rainbow for a mouth. It eeyored twice to mark the half-hour and Surinder's timetable flapped straight out of the rose-tinted window as he beheld Topaz's lilac moustache and the tawny pony-tail springing out of one ear. And his heart jerked and boinged in time to the grand piano which at that moment struck up an improvised tune to 'Carrots Cleaning Their Teeth'. For Surinder Sewing Machine Singh and Topaz Matilda-Jane Smith, time simply stood still.

That night Surinder's father yelled up the stairs to say that they were five, eight, twelve, *fifteen* minutes into 'News at Ten' and Surinder's Relaxing Drink had developed a skin. Surinder, however, was busy explaining to Delroy that he wasn't going to be a brain surgeon after all but would be owning a whole chain of jewellers' shops instead. In each of his stores he would be dedicating an entire window to displaying a single gem and in every one there would be a scroll curling out of a broken alarm clock, emblazoned with the device 'A Topaz is For Ever ...' His father hollered up the stairs for absolutely the last time to recall to his son's mind the grave importance of keeping up with World Events. But Surinder didn't even hear him as he started his fourth closely-packed page to his Birmingham friend ...

Thinking it over

1 What would you say the story is essentially about? There are at least three or four possible answers. Put them in the order that means most to you. Then, discuss your answers in a group and see if it is possible for all your group to agree on the order of importance.

2 What is your final impression of the two central characters — Surinder and Topaz? Write pen-portraits of them of not more than 100 words. Then, form groups and discuss what you have written. Whose pen-portrait captures (a) Surinder, (b) Topaz most accurately?

3 What do you think Surinder's and Topaz's school reports would be like? Based on the information given in the story and the mental pictures you have built up of them, write a school report for one of them. Then, in groups discuss what you have written and why.

4 The story gives detailed descriptions of Surinder's bedroom and of Topaz's living-room. Why does the author describe them in such detail?

Either draw a plan or a picture of Surinder's bedroom or Topaz's living-room based on the information given in the story or imagine what you think Topaz's bedroom would be like and draw a picture or a diagram of it.

5 Talk about the part which the English lesson on Shakespeare's play *Macbeth* plays in the story. How important is it to know something about the play in order to be able to follow the story? Discuss any of the references to the play which you found hard to understand.

6 How would you sum up your reaction to the story? Did you find it amusing? boring? realistic? unconvincing? effective? silly? informative? Write a brief statement saying what you thought of the story, then form groups and discuss your opinion of the story.

Role play

Guess what happened today
Either imagine that instead of writing a letter to Delroy that evening, Surinder decides to ring him up; *or* imagine that Topaz has a close friend. That evening she goes round to see her. In pairs, act out one of the conversations that takes place.

How the author tells the story

1 Susan Gregory often writes stories about children with Asian or West Indian backgrounds. If you decide to write about people from a different culture to your own, you must avoid presenting a stereotyped view of their culture. How successful do you think Susan Gregory is in depicting her two heroes and their backgrounds? (Note: You can read more of Susan

Gregory's stories in the collection *Martini-on-the-rocks*, published by Puffin.)

2 a) Although the story is written in the third person, the events are presented very much from Surinder's point of view. Why do you think Susan Gregory chose to write in the third person rather than the first person? Try rewriting the first two paragraphs in the first person and see whether or not it works better.

b) One theme in the story is letter-writing. The story could even have been written in the form of a sequence of letters between the two boys. Try rewriting the story as a series of letters describing these events. What will Delroy's role be?

4: Only a kid

MARK PETERS

She yelled at me. 'Get the b-u-c-k-e-t.' I didn't know what she wanted. 'Disobedient boy,' she said to me as a Greek kid handed her the red plastic thing that had been in the corner.

Aqualife stinks if you ask me. I could catch those fish with my bare hands and in my country we used to have a pond with hundreds of fish which I had to look after. Miss makes us write all sorts of things about fish in our books.

Anyway I don't like fish. I only chose this subject because the girl from Timor is in the class.

Yesterday, the Greek kids who live near my place called out

bad things to me when I walked past their house. There must have been at least eight of them in the garden and on the footpath. My friend at the tech college had a big fight with the Turkish kids there. I should buy a knife and then I'd show them.

The girl from Timor is very nice. I can't say her name; it is too hard for me. Some Ock names are hard to say but hers is more difficult. Ock means Australian in my language.

I came here two years ago. I didn't want to leave my country but my parents made me. I live with my brother and his two children. Sometimes I miss my mum and dad very much. Now my dad is getting old. My brother's wife is still in our country. My brother has sponsored her and she will come here next year, maybe.

Hieu is going to Perth. He lived with his brother who didn't give him any money. When his brother's wife came she did not like Hieu. They have a car, and his brother and his wife and their children used to go away and leave Hieu by himself. He was very unhappy. Now he is going to Perth by himself because he has a friend there and his friend said Hieu could live with him.

The girl from Timor talked to me yesterday. She asked me why I didn't wait for her after school and walk with her. When she smiles she is very nice. I think she is better than my old girl friend. Sometimes the girl from Timor won't look at me and sometimes she smiles at me. I don't understand. When she won't talk to me I am very sad.

I don't like school. The kids don't like me. Often they say, 'Ching-chong, Ching-chong' to me. But I am not Chinese.

Last term I got into trouble with my maths teacher. When he gave me my report he told my brother that I talk to Pham during all his lessons. It's not true. I never talk to Pham. My brother was very angry with me. He blamed me and said that I was a lazy boy. I think that our maths teacher thinks all blackhairs look the same.

At school we have excursions and things. My brother doesn't like me to go because he thinks I should work at school. Every night he tells me to do my homework and does not believe me when I say that I have none. He did not stay at school too long but thinks that kids should work all the time. My friends get more money than me and none of them has to cook dinner for a family every night when they get home from school. I always have to cook for my brother and his two children and I am only a kid. I never cooked in my country and had to begin when I came here. Sometimes I like to cook things and sometimes I hate it. My brother is often angry with me if I go to practise soccer after school and come home late to cook. My brother always works overtime. He has to save money for his wife, to buy a car when she comes and to pay for a house. He says that his boss is angry with him if he can't work overtime. He works in a factory.

Tonight I waited for the girl from Timor after school. I waited with my friend Hy. He has a new bike. His father died when they escaped from my country and now he lives with his mother. She sews clothes at home on a big sewing machine. They have a video. She is always working.

The girl from Timor came out of the schoolground with some boys and girls from her class. One of the boys said hello to me. I knew him in the refugee camp. The girl would not look at me or speak to me. I had to pretend that I was waiting for someone else. Then I did not speak to Hy again and I came home.

Tonight I cooked again and now I am going to bed. My brother blamed me tonight because he saw me writing a poem in my language and said that I should be doing my homework. I have no homework and I want to sleep.

Thinking it over

1 How did you feel as you read this story? Did you identify with the boy and feel sympathy for him? Did you find it a moving story?

2 This is a very different type of story from the previous three stories. In what ways is it different from them? What sort of story would you say it is?

3 The story is set in Australia. Do you think it is an autobiographical story and that Mark Peters actually is the boy in the story? Give your reasons.

4 How old do you think the boy in the story is? Where do you think he comes from? List the important facts about the boy that you are told in the story. Then, list any important facts about him which you are not told. Why do you think the author chose to include certain facts but not others?

5 What are the boy's feelings about his life in Australia? Select one paragraph because you think it conveys very clearly what he feels. Then, discuss in a group which paragraph you chose and why.

6 Talk about the title of the story. Do you think it is an effective title? Suggest an alternative title.

Role play

Starting a new life
A TV company is making a documentary about children who have recently moved to Australia. Work in pairs and act out a scene in which a reporter interviews the boy. Before you begin, make a list of the questions the interviewer is going to ask the boy and discuss how you think the boy will answer them.

How the author tells the story

1 The story is told as a first person narrative. It is as if the boy is writing down his thoughts. He starts telling us about some of the things that have happened to him in the past two days and, as he does so, other thoughts cross his mind, so he tells us about them too. Work in pairs. Talk about the structure of the story. Try to draw a flow chart or diagram showing how the story is structured.

2 What do you notice about the style of language used in this story? Try writing a story about the experiences of someone who has to begin a new life in a different country, perhaps because she/he is a refugee. See if you can use your writing style, as Mark Peters does, to suggest the way the person uses language. But be careful not to exaggerate or you will lose your reader's sympathy.

5: Belfast Saturday

JENNI RUSSELL

Bomb Blast: Five Feared Dead

CATHOLIC WOMAN FIGHTS OFF ATTACKER

SINN FEIN SAYS TROOPS OUT

Pub Bomb: Two Held

CAR BOMB KILLS UDR MAN

Seven o'clock.

Grey-haired Mrs Collins turned over in her bed, a huge mountain of flesh. The room was stuffy, but she could not open the window because the lock was broken, and there was no one to mend it since 'He' had died six years ago.

Her alarm-clock went off promptly at seven-five, and she slowly heaved her massive bulk out from underneath the bedclothes. She dressed herself slowly, shivering in the cold of the unheated room.

Miss Jeanie O'Flaherty had been up for an hour already. Tonight her boyfriend was taking her out, and she had been up early, pressing and ironing her best clothes.

Jeanie looked appraisingly at her reflection in the full-length mirror. She smiled suddenly at herself, then stood stock-still, listening, as she heard the faint rattle of gunfire.

'How far away?' she breathed to herself, hoping desperately, 'not here, Lord, not here, not again.' Last week she had seen a car pass and had watched, helpless, as two young teenage boys were mowed down with bullets. She was shaking now, re-living the terror of that moment, hearing the one boy's scream of agony, watching the other drop to the ground without uttering a sound.

Mrs Collins munched her cornflakes while she listened dispassionately to the news.

'... and these murders bring Ulster's civilian death toll to 637, since 1969. Now for the weather.'

She switched the radio off, and continued to eat. Mrs Collins had never been actively involved in the violence, and after the first shocks, when deaths were announced daily, she accepted everything with stoicism.

Fifteen minutes later, she was down on her knees, scrubbing the kitchen floor. Sean Collins had always liked a clean house. His photograph stood on top of the green wooden table in the corner of the room. She was glad that he had not lived to see 'these awful goings-on' as she termed it in her mind.

Breathing heavily, she pulled herself to her feet, took a duster, and polished, gently, the silver photograph frame. Sean Collins's face smiled up at her as she worked.

Carefully she replaced the photograph, and moved on to tidy her minute front-room.

There was nothing to tidy. She ran her duster quickly over the furniture, and sat down to rest in one of the uncomfortable armchairs. The last time any visitor had been in here, she recalled, was when the vicar came to tell her that Sean was dead.

Jeanie was washing up. Her next-door neighbour, Brigit Maloney, Jeanie's own age, was talking eagerly about make-up and dresses. Jeanie placed the last plate in the rack.

'Come upstairs, Brigit, I've laid out my clothes for this afternoon. Andrew's taking me out, you know.'

Brigit admired Jeanie's new dress, which was white-bordered with blue stripes. Jeanie was wearing it now, turning round and round slowly.

'Oh, won't you look lovely tonight!' Brigit breathed. 'Have you any blue eye-shadow? It would go with that ever so well!'

Jeanie shook her head. 'I couldn't afford it before, but I've been saving for three weeks, and I'm going to buy it this afternoon.'

Ten minutes to two.

Mrs Collins, retired charwoman, grey-haired and humble, was out shopping at the nearby supermarket. She peered anxiously at Campbell's Soups, threepence off recommended price, or should she buy a packet soup, penny cheaper? She was pondering on the question, when she heard a shrill voice exclaiming:

'Look, Mum, that lady's dress is darned!'

Mrs Collins wished she could disappear. Pretending to be oblivious of the many faces turned in her direction, she continued staring at the soups, but she had never felt so flustered inside since, as a child, she had been made to stand on a stool in front of the school in disgrace.

Miss Jeanie O'Flaherty, shop assistant, off-duty, black-haired and strongly Catholic, looked sympathetically at the old woman, smoothing down her own blue dress while she did so. At three o'clock her boyfriend was coming to take her out, and Jeanie had bought a new dress for the occasion. Now she was running over the merits of different types of make-up in her mind. Only ten shillings to spend, and so many different kinds of lipstick, eye-shadow, cheek-shiner and nail-varnish! Perhaps after all she had better buy that 'Glamor Girl' make-up box. It was *so* hard to decide — Jeanie glanced at the time. Five minutes to two.

Mrs Collins had decided on Campbell's Soups. After all, Sean had always preferred tinned soup when they could afford it, and besides, her grandchildren were coming to tea, little Mark, Barbara and Johnny. She thought affectionately of Barbara, nice little girl that she was, well-mannered and always polite — one of the reasons for visiting the supermarket was to buy a present for Barbara, whose birthday was in two days' time. Mrs Collins had saved for a month to be able to afford buying her granddaughter the eleven-shilling doll she wanted.

The old lady glanced down at her unpolished shoes, and wondered if she could afford just a tiny tin of shoe-polish. Mrs Collins found life hard these days, living on a minute pension while prices of goods grew higher and higher.

Jeanie stopped in front of a mirror and patted her hair into place. She looked unseeingly at the mirror, as her boyfriend told her that she was the most beautiful girl in the world. Then she was literally brought down to earth, as Mrs Collins walked into her. 'Sorry,' Mrs Collins said, and Jeanie was just scrambling to her feet, when—

Two o'clock.

The rescue workers dug for three hours before uncovering the bodies. Enough was left of Mrs Collins to be identified, but all that remained of Jeanie was a pile of ashes and a scrap of blue material fluttering forlornly in the wind—

Thinking it over

1 Which of the two characters were you able to visualise most clearly? Talk about the details of (a) Mrs Collins's (b) Jeanie's physical appearance and clothes which are described in the story.

2 Talk about how Mrs Collins is presented.
   a) What information are you given about Mrs Collins's background? How is it conveyed?
   b) What do you learn about Mrs Collins from the way she spends her day? What do you learn about her from the sort of things she says?

3 Talk about how Jeanie is presented.
   a) What do you learn about Jeanie's background?
   b) What does she spend her day doing and what thoughts occupy her mind?

4 Compare Jeanie's lifestyle with Mrs Collins's lifestyle. How would you sum up their different lifestyles? Do you think the story would have been more or less effective if one of the two characters had been totally different — for example if, instead of Jeanie, the other main character had been a middle-aged businessman?

5 Discuss the ending of the story. Was it entirely a surprise? How effectively does the writer introduce the background of Ulster and the troubles there? How is the tension built up?

Role play

Belfast Bomb Blast — Two Dead
Work in pairs. One of you is a TV reporter, the other is either an eye-witness and/or a friend or relative of either Jeanie or

Mrs Collins. Develop a television news report giving details of the explosion and of the two dead people and containing an interview with an eye-witness and/or someone who knew either Jeanie or Mrs Collins.

How the author tells the story

1 a) Discuss how this story is constructed. Draw a diagram to show how the plot develops and comes to its climax. (Note: There are several ways in which you could choose to show this.)

b) You could use a similar structure for any 'action' story of your own. Use the diagram to help you as you plan, think of a different context and tell your own story leading up to a climactic event.

2 You can learn a lot from this story about how to present characters in stories. Young writers often concentrate too much on describing a person's physical appearance and their clothes, instead of building up a picture of a person's lifestyle by telling the reader about their background and their habits, and by describing what the person thinks, says and does. Bearing this in mind, (a) write a short story in which you attempt to convey what a person is like by describing a typical day in her/his life; or (b) alternatively, use *Belfast Saturday* as a model and write a story about two people during a single day in which they come together for some reason at the end of the story. The reason need not be a dramatic event such as a bomb explosion. They could be introduced to each other at a party, stand next to one another in a queue or meet in a waiting room.

6: No holier than thou

JOHN GRIFFIN

Billy Ossett and me had three secrets. The first was about Jim Dickinson, a shepherd, the next was about Mr Cockburn, the curate, and the third was about us. We didn't tell any of these secrets because they were all nasty ones, that would get us into trouble.

Billy Ossett had a ferret called Killer. Killer was scared of rabbits, which was a handicap for a ferret. One March morning we spent two hours trying to make Killer go down a rabbit hole. In the end Billy pushed him down as far as his hand could reach and then put his old blue jumper over the hole to stop him popping up. After ten minutes he took the jumper away and, sure enough, Killer had disappeared.

'He'll be up with one in a minute,' said Billy. His pink little face was creased in the smile of pride he always had when telling us what Killer could do.

An hour later there was still no sign of Killer. He'd obviously either gone to sleep or been savaged by a bunny. We abandoned him and went home.

'We'll fetch him tonight,' said Billy. 'He's bound to come up when he gets hungry.'

About ten o'clock I was just getting off to sleep when a stone hit my bedroom window. I looked out and thought I saw a carpet wriggling on the ground. Then the carpet stood up and proved to be Billy Ossett wearing his dad's overcoat. He'd found another stone and was about to launch it.

'All right, I'm coming,' I hissed down at him. I didn't want to go but I knew if Billy was determined he was quite capable of heaving half a brick through my window.

Clouds were scudding across the moon as we made our way up the hedgerows, so it was alternately dark and light. When we reached the rabbit hole Killer was sniffing about at the top.

'Told you,' said Billy, triumphantly and popped Killer in his basket.

'Let's have a chat with Jim in his hut,' said Billy, feeling big after his success in finding Killer so easily.

Jim Dickinson was a friendly young shepherd who worked for Colonel Smithers. In the early spring he had to stay with his flock all night till the lambs were strong enough to look after themselves. Jim's hut was only two hundred yards away. It was made of corrugated iron and had no windows.

'Perhaps he's out lambing,' I said. 'We'll knock on his door.'

'Let's have a look if he's in first,' said Billy and squinted through one of the many chinks in the corrugated iron. I looked through another chink. It was a filthy place, lit by a paraffin lamp in the corner. There were a few tools and old coats hanging from the cobwebby walls and a straw mattress covered by a couple of beet pulp bags. I could see Jim. He was lying under the beet bags. And there was somebody under them with him. Billy and I stared for a minute and then we turned and ran. Billy's feet were hidden by his dad's overcoat and so he lost control of them and tripped in a rabbit hole. He yelled and we paused for breath.

'That's Mrs Maxwell in there,' said Billy.

'I know,' I said. 'What's she doing there?'

'Lovin' I reckon,' said Billy and giggled.

His giggle was cut short by Jim's boot up his backside. He must have heard Billy's yell and sneaked out to find us.

'Hello, Jim,' I said, trying to sound friendly.

Jim grabbed my hair, yanked me back and chucked me on the ground next to Billy. Then he kicked us both, really hard kicks.

'What's up with you?' I said, starting to cry.

Jim looked at us both carefully. The moon was quite bright and I could see his face clearly. It was full of hate and fear.

'If you ever say a word to anybody about coming up here I'll strangle you both,' he said.

He gave us another kick and went back to his hut.

We staggered home.

'I ain't going to say anything about it,' said Billy. 'He's loopy. He'd do us in.'

I knew Billy was right. Every time I saw Jim, Mrs Maxwell or her husband Joe, who was the school caretaker, I thought about that night. But I never told anybody. Jim seemed to have forgotten all about it. He was his usual friendly self whenever I met him.

Another friendly person was Mr Cockburn, a timid little

chap of about twenty, with black hair and a pasty face. He was the curate, a sort of apprentice vicar. Foster-Pegg was the proper vicar. He was old, fierce and scraggy. After church one Sunday Foster-Pegg said,

'I'm starting a church youth club in the Reading Room. It will be every Friday at seven o'clock. Mr Cockburn will be in charge.'

That was quite good news to us. You could see from his face it was also news to poor old Cockburn — bad news. He couldn't control us at choir-practice so there wasn't much chance of him controlling us at a youth club.

'But what about ... er ... equipment, sir?' said Cockburn.

'You'll find a way. I've every confidence in you,' said Foster-Pegg and walked off. You could tell by the way he said it he hadn't any confidence at all and wanted to upset him as much as he could.

He succeeded. We started off with ping-pong, darts and a little snooker table. Within three weeks poor old Cockburn was cowering in the corner while we belted around the Reading Room playing football with ping-pong balls.

'Steady boys, be careful, now,' Cockburn used to say as the noise and the tackles grew more ferocious. While it lasted this Youth Club was the most dangerous place I've ever been in. You had to keep careful watch on the flying boots and keep your head fairly low to avoid the flying missiles — Needham's darts. While most of us cluttered round the oak-panelled room, pursuing the ping-pong balls Needham pursued his personal ambition of scoring treble twenty from thirty feet — one end of the Reading Room to the other. Of course he had to launch his darts like javelins and after one had parted the goalkeeper's hair Cockburn tried to put his foot down.

'Don't you think that's rather dangerous, Eric?' he said to Needham.

'Naw,' said Needham.

'I don't want to see any accidents,' said Cockburn bravely.

'Go down the pub; then you won't see anything,' said Needham, and launched another dart which stuck in the ceiling. There was a rumour that Cockburn used to drink a lot and Needham and Fatty often told him to go down the pub if he complained too much.

Then one night the Youth Club ended with a bang — a bang of Fatty Hardcastle's head on the War Memorial board, as he tried to stop the ping-pong ball going through his goal — the open door leading to the kitchen part. Fatty's head was undamaged — nothing could hurt that part of him — but the oak board, with all the names of village blokes who'd been killed in the war, split and a lump fell off.

At the bottom of the board there was a poem that was called 'For the Fallen'. Most of this had fallen off. We were just trying to nail it back on, with poor old Cockburn panicking and squeaking like a hen in a fit, when Foster-Pegg arrived. There was a dead silence. Fatty tried to conceal the broken board with his fatness, but Foster-Pegg was not fooled. We were all sent home in disgrace. But we weren't as disgraced as Cockburn.

'Perhaps you'll stay behind and furnish me with an explanation of this disgraceful scene,' Foster-Pegg said to him nastily.

We left poor old Cockburn to it. I was secretly relieved. Going to the Youth Club had become like going to war. If it had gone on much longer there would have been a memorial for the Youth Club fallen.

Next Sunday after choir, Foster-Pegg said,

'It seems you are not civilised enough to behave in a Youth Club. Some outdoor activity will suit you better. Mr Cockburn will organise a weekend's camping, beginning on Thursday and returning in time for Evensong.'

Of course this wasn't so much an outing for us as a punishment for Cockburn.

The camp was only a mile and a half from the village. We lugged the old army tents Cockburn had hired to the site and settled down to enjoy ourselves, mostly at poor old Cockburn's expense. It took three hours to erect the tents, mainly because while old Cockburn was threshing about under the canvas like a dog with colic, trying to erect them from the inside, we were 'helping' him by standing on the edges of the canvas so he couldn't get out.

After two nights of chaos Foster-Pegg turned up, probably hoping we'd finished old Cockburn off. When he saw the haggard red-eyed sleepless face, he smiled quietly in satisfaction. Then he said Cockburn could go off for a rest while he took over — he wanted to show him how easy it was to control us. We helped Foster-Pegg put up his fancy blue tent a decent distance from the rest. This time we really helped, because we were scared of him.

Not as scared as Billy and I were, though, in the middle of the night when we were woken by this scratching noise.

'I bet it's a rat,' said Billy, who was as scared of rats as Killer was of rabbits.

It was Cockburn. His white face with bloodshot eyes stuck itself through the tent flap.

'Oh dear, wrong tent,' he said and scuttled off.

'He's drunk,' said Billy.

'Easy is,' I said.

His voice had been all slurry and he'd had to hold on to the tent to stand up.

We pulled on our wellies and followed him. He was staggering from tent to tent, checking them all. I got hold of his arm.

'Yours is there,' I said, pointing to his little tent near the tree.

'I'm not looking for my tent,' he slurred. 'I'm looking for that Foster-Pegg, that Philistine, that hypocrite. I shall smite him down.'

Then he caught sight of Foster-Pegg's fancy tent and lurched towards it.

'Best not,' I said, trying to steer him away.

He looked at me puzzled.

'You're right,' he said suddenly. 'Vengeance is the Lord's, not mine. I'll wee on him instead.'

Billy and me watched amazed and giggling as he stationed himself in front of the blue tent and let fly a fountain all over it.

We giggled ourselves to sleep eventually. In the morning everything was normal. Maybe old Foster-Pegg thought it was funny that there had been a storm in the night that had only wet his tent. Perhaps he thought God had picked him out specially for a shower. But he didn't mention it.

Cockburn did though. Billy and I were collecting wood when Cockburn came up to us, his face white and fierce.

'I've got the right two boys, haven't I?' he said.

We didn't say anything.

'I'm not sure what I said or did last night, but I think I remember. Whatever it was, I must ask you not to repeat it to anyone. Do you understand?'

'Yes, sir,' said Billy.

And we never did. I never thought I'd be scared of Cockburn, but what he'd done had made him fierce.

'He'll get us if we tell,' I explained to Billy.

'I know that,' said Billy. 'You've only got to look in his face.'

Somehow I didn't like Jim Dickinson or Cockburn for what they'd done to us. After all, it wasn't our fault that we caught them out. I understood how they felt though when I nearly killed Ian Thorne, a few weeks after he'd come to the village when his dad took over the White Swan.

In the winter we used to sledge down Church Hill. It was a

gentle slope but three fields long. If you steered your sledge between the two gaps in the hedges you could complete the whole course without getting off. All our sledges went about the same speed—they were all home-made from bits of old wood with iron runners.

This Ian had a big green sledge that he called a toboggan—bought from a shop in town. He was a friendly kid, but we didn't like him, because his sledge went much faster than ours.

The most exciting sledging was in the dark. You could just see, even on moonless nights, until you got to the gaps in the hedges. It was very dark there but we managed to mark the gaps with lanterns. If you steered between them you were safe.

One January night the snow was just right for sledging. Even our home-made machines were going quite fast. But Ian Thorne was always at the bottom before us, except when he lent one of us his sledge, which he often did. About half-past eight we set off on our last run. We were speeding along through the second field when we passed Ian, dragging his sledge back up, having got down well before us.

'I'll just have another run,' he shouted as we went by. 'I'll easy catch you up.'

Well, it wasn't much of a brag, if it was a brag at all, and anyway it was certainly true. But as we started to pull our sledges back up, knowing that we'd had the excitement for the day, and all we had left was the long slog up the hill and, most probably, a clip round the ear for being out so late, we felt fed-up.

'That Ian's a big-head,' said Billy.

'You heard what he said, didn't you?' I asked.

'Yea, he'll catch us up easy. Big-headed snob,' said Billy.

'My dad says the pub's gone downhill since his dad took over,' said Fatty. Fatty's dad was in the best position to judge the pub, since he spent every night in it.

'Let's knock him off his sledge when he comes by,' said Billy.

'He'd more likely knock us,' said Fatty.

We were nearing the gap in the hedge when I had a sudden inspiration.

'I know, let's move the lanterns.'

We moved the lanterns so there was a tree in the middle of them. We waited anxiously, each of us hoping it wouldn't work, but none of us daring to chicken out now we'd done it. Ian hit the tree with a sickening thump. He rolled off and lay still in the snow. The side of his sledge that hit the tree came off, and the rest of it careered away, crippled as its owner, down the hill.

He started to come round after about five minutes, making moaning noises at first and struggling with his feet.

'It's your fault,' said Billy to me.

'Who moved the lanterns?' I shouted angrily.

'Don't matter about that,' said Fatty who had moved one of the lanterns. 'You suggested it. It was a rotten trick.'

I knew that all right and it made me mad.

'Listen,' I said desperately, 'you helped me do it. We've gotta make him say it was an accident.'

We sat Ian up. He was coming round all right now. He had a gash on his head, and his nose was bleeding. He looked round at us, at the tree, and then the lanterns.

'You moved the lanterns,' he croaked.

'Are you all right?' asked Fatty, trying to fix a friendly smile on his pudding face.

'You moved the lanterns,' Ian said again. And then he said it over and over like a gramophone that's stuck.

'Listen you. You listen to me,' I said fiercely. 'It was an accident. You hit a bump and the sledge veered off into that tree.'

'Not my sledge,' he said with a touch of pride. 'You moved the lanterns.'

'Just you shut your gob saying that,' said Fatty, abandoning his smile. 'If you say that again, ever again, to anybody, you've had it. Do you understand that?'

Ian understood all right. And as soon as he understood we started to be nice to him. We sorted him out as best we could, tried to mend his sledge and took him home to explain about his 'accident'.

He was all right in a few days. In fact he was all right as a kid. He didn't say anything and you can be sure none of us did.

Well, after that I understood all about Jim Dickinson and Cockburn. I even understand how Killer was scared of rabbits. Rabbits, worms, Jims and even Cockburns will turn nasty if you get them cornered.

Thinking it over

1 Within this story there are accounts of three separate incidents. Talk about what happens in each one. Try to think of a suitable heading or title for each separate account, which appropriately sums up what happens in that particular incident.

2 a) As you read the story were you worried about the lack of continuity between the separate events?

b) Talk about the ending. Did the final paragraph help you to tie the whole story together? Did you feel you needed to turn back and re-read some parts to see how everything fitted in?

3 The story is presented as a first-person narrative, so we see the events from the author's and Billy's point of view. Does that mean that your sympathies always lie with them? Talk about each incident in turn. Who did you sympathise with most — the author and Billy or (a) Jim (b) Mr Cockburn (c) Ian. Say why.

4 'An amusing story with a sting in the tail.' Discuss this view of the story. How would you sum up your reaction to the story? Write two or three sentences saying what you thought of the story, then form groups and discuss what you have written.

5 An alternative title for the story would be 'Secrets'. Which do you think is a better title — 'Secrets' or 'No holier than thou'? Explain why.

Role play

You keep your mouth shut, or else!
In groups, act out a scene in which a group of children warn a girl or boy that she/he had better not say anything about what has happened or they'll be for it.

How the author tells the story

1 As you read the story what were you thinking of? Often when we read a story it sets us thinking about things that have happened to us, so that while we are still following the events of the story, at the same time we are making connections between the story and our own lives. Did this story remind you of any secrets you have had to keep, of any nasty incidents you have been involved in or of times when you have been warned to keep your mouth shut? Or perhaps it reminded you of other stories you have read, seen or heard? Writers draw on their own experiences or on stories they have heard to provide them with ideas for their stories. Did this story provide you with a memory or an idea that could form the basis of a story? Make some notes about what you were thinking of as you read this story. See if you can use them to develop a story of your own. Remember, if your story is based on a memory you need not stick exactly to what happened. Reshape the events to fit the story you want to tell.

2 Plot out a story which, like *No Holier Than Thou*, has a number of separate incidents in it. Make sure that the incidents are connected in some way, just as in John Griffin's story the incidents are connected by the explanation at the end. Before you write your story, form groups and discuss your plots. Be prepared to listen to suggestions and to alter your plot if anyone suggests ideas which you think would improve it.

7: The light in the dark

ROBERT MORGAN

1

Sometimes he was seen coming down from the mountain on late evenings. He went to the mountain for solitude to damp his confusing, sullen moods. He was a boy of seventeen, a strange boy, with large, brown, sad eyes, unkempt hair and an awkward gait due to self-consciousness. He kept to himself, living on the edge of the community like a tamed wild bird that reappeared, now and then, for food and shelter.

Old Tom Williams, who lived in the corner house in Church Street, owned a dog that went off for days on end. When it returned to the house, bedraggled and weary, it curled itself up under a chair, stared at the old man, then fell asleep. The old man used to wonder where it had been and he thought the dog strange. The boy was something like old Tom's dog. At the far end of the village, Will Mason, who had been decorated in the First World War, kept a secondhand clothes shop. The front of the shop hadn't been painted for years, and gave the impression of an old, cracked, leather-covered book, but everyone had got used to it looking like that, just as everyone had got used to the boy and his desire to be disconnected from the life of the village.

The boy lived with his mother, a widow, in a terraced cottage surrounded by colliers and their families. When the boy was in his seventh year he had been awakened in the middle of the night by a loud knocking on the front door, and creeping downstairs he had witnessed the lifeless, coalblack body of his father brought home from the pit by his workmates. The image of his father often came to him in his solitary walks to the mountain, but however hard he tried he could not get the image clear in his imagination.

The village, set in a deep narrow valley, was built for the convenience of the low seam pit, and the terraced streets, in long curved rows, like giant steps, sloped down to a black river and railway lines. The main road had a dozen shops, and at several corners of terraces, above and below the main road, were enormous chapel buildings plain and grey. From the pit surface, on an aerial railway, buckets of slag moved slowly on a steel rope towards a black cone on the summit of a mountain.

The boy's mother, Eliza Hughes, was an active, nervous woman, constantly on the move, work-conscious and domineering in a quiet way. She had seen better times, having had for a grandfather a Baptist Minister, who had been something of a scholar with several published essays to his credit. Her father, a farrier, had brought her from North Wales to the

Glamorgan Mining Valley, leaving behind a beautiful cwm with a clean, sparkling river and memories of her kind, gentle grandfather officiating in a chapel among trees and meadows.

Eliza had never forgotten her past life in the rural setting of North Wales. Her family had been something then. Her grandfather had owned a pony-and-trap and she had vivid memories of riding with him during his town visits. Eliza still carried herself as if she belonged to a better class, and the women in the pit village secretly envied her superior bearing and manner. When her parents returned to North Wales she remained and married Tom Hughes, a miner. She was immensely happy, for her husband was dashing and strong, with a shock of dark, curly hair that was the envy of every woman; but as the years passed, her romantic feelings and thoughts turned sour, for her husband neglected her, bored her, and spent much of his time in the local pubs drinking with his workmates. She saw in him a man of no ambition and no substance and she grew away from him. When he was killed in the pit she only felt a numbness, followed by a sense of relief. This episode drew her closer to her son and she had gone to a great deal of trouble shielding him from the storms of adolescence, so that the boy's nature was flowering on a nervous base. Consequently he was always on the lookout for dangers, and he feared the strong, boisterous pit youths around him. He was always being afraid of something. He was like a deer feeding in the clearing of a forest.

Eliza looked upon her son with proud feelings. She saw he wasn't coarse like his father had been, or like the youths who worked down the pit. Perhaps, she thought, he would become like her grandfather and move people with words and the example of his life. She proudly watched him grow into a youth and prayed he would become something special; but she also noticed he had grown handsome, having almost the exact features of his father, and the same dark, curly hair.

Secretly and often the boy visited the pit where his father had worked, where the rough, boisterous youths went each day to battle against the elements of rock, coal and danger. He envied the pit youths; they took life in strides, took it by the scruff of the neck and enjoyed it. He felt life should be treated like that, but he had no idea how to grip hold of it and enjoy it himself. Often he felt like a prisoner between the valley mountains. If only he could stretch out, he thought, and take hold of life like those around him.

The boy's name was Ivor, named after the Baptist preacher. He worked in the village ironmonger's shop, not far from his home. He often gave the wrong change and overweight on the scales, and the owner, a local Councillor by the name of Moses, who was a formal man, religious and avaricious, reprimanded the boy on several occasions in the presence of customers. The boy was almost sick with embarrassment during these reprimands and he was always unable to discuss the problem with his mother. For days afterwards he would wring his hands and hated returning to the smells of paraffin, paint, putty and the towering Moses.

There was always a reserved relationship between the mother and son. She seemed always before him, important, confident and busy. Sometimes during the long summer evenings he would go to his bedroom on the pretext of turning in early. From the bedroom window he had a view of the pit at which he would stare as if in a trance. The black iron framework stood solid and impressive, like a great iron fist over the village. How he wished he could stand up like that so that everyone could see him and not be afraid. It seemed to him his father had once stood like that, solid, impressive, challenging life with his hands. Sometimes the boy stood watching until darkness fell over the black iron frame, and in the darkness he seemed to feel its presence as it vibrated its quiet nightshift song. When he moved about in his room his mother would listen, trying to interpret the sounds as some kind of revolt against her. She fidgeted when she heard him move about, for the sounds were like words against her. Several times she was on the verge of climbing the stairs to his room to console and reprimand him, but she lost courage at the last moment.

2

In the same village as Ivor lived a girl whose name was Ruth. She was an attractive girl, strong-willed and intelligent. She worked as an assistant at the Indian and China Tea Company, a clean little shop opposite the ironmonger's. Ruth was very efficient, tactful with customers and as fresh as a spring flower in her white shop coat. She added up grocery bills swiftly and accurately in the old-fashioned way, and her handwriting and figures were confident, neat and beautifully shaped. Ruth often spoke to Ivor across the street when he was arranging the miner's tools on the pavement by the shop windows. He seldom spoke to her, but stared in silence whenever she called across to him. She was curious about Ivor's peculiar behaviour and very much aware of his handsome features and dark curly hair.

Ruth was crazy about dancing, having frequented every dance hall in the valley at one time or another. One evening she was returning home from a dance hall in the next village, taking a short cut from the bus stop towards her home which was in one of the top terraces nearest the mountain. Ivor, on one of his solitary journeys, had climbed down from the mountain and he was making his way towards the pit. The evening was quiet except for the distant chug and swish of the compressor unit on the pit surface. It was getting dark, the daylight changing into moonlight with darkness spreading thickly over the ground. The boy's head was full of racing thoughts and an idea was beginning to form in his mind. As he walked along he began to feel exhilarated in the warm summer air. He glanced at the moon taking over the last of the daylight and he began to feel free of his prison. Alone in the semi-darkness and stimulated by his thoughts he began to talk to himself.

'When my father was in the darkness of the pit he must have felt like this', he muttered. 'He was not afraid . . . and he must have died without fear, fighting it with his bare hands. His death is an example to me . . . I know it is.'

His soliloquy was disturbed by the appearance of Ruth, who almost walked into him in the moonlight.

'Ivor!' she called out in a frightened voice, 'It's you!'

He was embarrassed and just looked at her without speaking.

'Where are you going this time of night?' she asked.

'For a walk,' he muttered.

'I'll come with you.'

'If you like,' he said hesitatingly.

'Don't say it like that Ivor boy; try and sound pleased. I turned down a half a dozen boys who wanted to take me home from the dance tonight.'

They walked on together, she talking and gesticulating with her delicate hands. He listened to her musical voice, repeating her confident words to himself. Suddenly she stopped, sat on the grass and looked up at the sky.

'Come and look at the stars with me, Ivor boy,' she said, 'what a lovely night it is!'

He wanted to speak, to say a great deal, but could not make the words come out of his mouth. She shook her head and wondered at his behaviour. He made his hands into fists to try and make himself speak.

'You're a strange boy, Ivor,' she mused, 'but it's not your

fault really. Your mother guards you like a cripple. Are you afraid of something? Why are you afraid?'

He saw her smile and struggled to unfold his hands. He wanted desperately to free them. He felt the pounding of his heart and a new excitement began to flower in the depth of his body. His fisted hands uncurled and he gripped her.

'What's come over you all of a sudden!' she uttered, surprised.

'I'm not afraid!' he said trembling, 'I'm not afraid . . . you'll see if I'm afraid or not!'

3

The village clock on top of the War Memorial struck 2 a.m. Gomer Thomas, banksman at the top of the pit, stood against the pit-gear lighting his pipe. He had just eaten his box of sandwiches, and in the calm, warm air outside his cabin he was quietly spending his snack-time. Above him a dust-caked electric bulb burned and several large moths fluttered around it. Out of the darkness Ivor appeared and stood in the glow of the electric light. Gomer stared at him for a moment, surprised at his appearance.

'Ivor boy!' Gomer called out, 'What on earth are you doing here at this time of night?'

'I've come to see the pit, that's all.'

'Well, well, what time of night is this to be looking at an ugly pit?'

Ivor gripped the metal framework of the pit-gear with both hands and felt the trembling, stiff, cold iron. His body caught the vibrations, giving him confidence.

'I always wanted to work down this pit, Gomer,' he continued. 'I always wanted to be like my father and work as a miner, but my mother forbade it. You knew my father, didn't you, Gomer? You knew him better than anyone.'

'Yes, you could say that.'

'What was he like, Gomer?'

'He was a good friend, a fine workman, and a strong, fearless man. I often saw him lift an empty tram on to the rails with his bare hands. He was a generous man and he would do anyone a favour. As boys we worked together in Owen's District. He was quite a lad in those days and in the dance hall he was as graceful on his feet as Fred Astaire. We started work on the same day down this pit, and we were always together in the old days.'

Gomer looked hard at the boy as he spoke.

'Have you been drinking, Ivor?' he asked casually.

'No, Gomer. I came here because I wanted to know something about my father, that's all. I've never heard anything good about him at home.'

Gomer lifted his cap and scratched his head, trying to sort out in his mind the odd behaviour of the boy in front of him. He noticed the striking resemblance between the boy and his father. It was like looking at his old friend.

The boy continued, 'You might not understand, Gomer, but I'm not afraid anymore. I want to be a miner like my father and come here to work every day like the other boys in our village.'

Under the electric light and the pit-gear the man and the boy talked for some length. When the boy left he had a clear image of his father and the life he led as a miner.

'I'm not afraid anymore,' he muttered as he walked towards the dark and silent village. 'I'll be like him, a miner. He was a strong and fearless man and I have been weak and afraid. I'll start work at the pit, for it's what I always wanted. It was she who started all this and I'm grateful to her. I'll ask her to marry me when I've settled everything with my mother.'

He touched his face where the girl's lips had been, and stumbled on into the darkness.

Thinking it over

1 What do you learn from the opening section of the story about Ivor's parents? What sort of person is his mother and how does she treat him?

2 Ivor is described as being different from the other villagers. In what ways is he different? What inner struggle is he battling with?

3 What part does Ruth play in the story? How does his meeting with Ruth enable Ivor to resolve his struggle and to make up his mind what he wants to do?

4 Why does Ivor go to see Gomer Thomas? What does he learn from Gomer that strengthens his resolve? What is he thinking and feeling as he walks home after talking to Gomer?

5 This story echoes some of the stories of D.H. Lawrence both in its theme and its setting. Like Lawrence, Robert Morgan grew up in a mining community. Discuss the details of the village that he includes in the story which enable us to picture clearly the background against which the events take place.

Role play

I've made up my mind
Act out the scene in which Ivor talks to his mother and announces to her what he plans to do.

How the author tells the story

1 a) In the opening section Robert Morgan uses a number of comparisons to help him to convey to the reader what Ivor is like. Talk about the comparisons he uses. Which of them did you find most effective, because it helped you to understand Ivor more clearly?

 b) Try to write one or two paragraphs in which you describe a person's character; for instance, you could describe someone who behaves in a rather brash, loud, apparently self-confident manner in order to cover up a basic insecurity. See if you can use one or two comparisons to help you to convey the impression you want to create.

2 a) Discuss how the story is structured in three sections. In the first section, Robert Morgan provides essential background information about Ivor, his family and the mining village in which he and his mother live. Then, in the second and third sections he describes two events that happen on the same evening, which together mark a turning-point in Ivor's life.

 b) See if you can structure a story in the same way. Begin with an introductory section which introduces the characters and sets the scene, then follow it with two or more sections in which something significant happens to one of the characters. Place your story in a setting which you can describe easily and accurately, because you know it from first-hand experience, in the way that Robert Morgan knows the mining village in which his story is set.

8: The darkness out there

PENELOPE LIVELY

She walked through flowers, the girl, ox-eye daisies and vetch and cow parsley, keeping to the track at the edge of the field. She could see the cottage in the distance, shrugged down into the dip beyond the next hedge. Mrs Rutter, Pat had said, Mrs Rutter at Nether Cottage, you don't know her, Sandra? She's a dear old thing, all on her own, of course, we try to keep an eye. A wonky leg after her op. and the home help's off with a bad back this week. So could you make that your Saturday afternoon session, dear? Lovely. There'll be one of the others, I'm not sure who.

Pat had a funny eye, asquint, so that her glance swerved away from you as she talked. And a big chest jutting under washed-out jerseys. Are people who help other people always not very nice-looking? Very busy being busy; always in a rush. You didn't get people like Mrs Carpenter at the King's Arms running the Good Neighbours' Club. People with platinum highlights and spike-heel suede boots.

She looked down at her own legs, the girl, bare brown legs brushing through the grass, polleny summer grass that glinted in the sun.

She hoped it would be Susie, the other person. Or Liz. They could have a good giggle, doing the floors and that. Doing her washing, this old Mrs Rutter.

They were all in the Good Neighbours' Club, her set at school. Quite a few of the boys, too. It had become a sort of craze, the thing to do. They were really nice, some of the old people. The old folks, Pat called them. Pat had done the notice in the library: 'Come and have fun giving a helping hand to the old folks. Adopt a granny.' And the jokey cartoon drawing of a dear old bod with specs on the end of her nose and a shawl. One or two of the old people had been a bit sharp about that.

The track followed the hedge round the field to the gate and the plank bridge over the stream. The dark reach of the spinney came right to the gate there so that she would have to walk by the edge of it with the light suddenly shutting off, the bare wide sky of the field. Packer's End.

You didn't go by yourself through Packer's End if you could help it, not after tea-time, anyway. A German plane came down in the war and the aircrew were killed and there were people who'd heard them talking still, chattering in German on their radios, voices coming out of the trees, nasty, creepy. People said.

She kept to the track, walking in the flowers with corn running in the wind between her and the spinney. She thought suddenly of blank-eyed helmeted heads, looking at you from among branches. She wouldn't go in there for a thousand pounds, not even in bright day like now, with nothing coming out of the dark slab of trees but bird-song — blackbirds and thrushes and robins and that. It was a rank place, all whippy saplings, and brambles and a gully with a dumped mattress and bedstead and an old fridge. And, somewhere, presumably, the crumbling rusty scraps of metal and cloth and ... bones?

It was all right out here in the sunshine. Fine. She stopped to pick grass stems out of her sandal; she saw the neat print of the strap-marks against her sunburn, pink-white on brown. Somebody had said she had pretty feet, once; she looked at them, clean and plump and neat on the grass. A ladybird crawled across a toe.

When they were small, six and seven and eight, they'd been scared stiff of Packer's End. Then, they hadn't known about the German plane. It was different things then; witches and wolves and tigers. Sometimes they'd go there for a dare, several of them, skittering over the field and into the edge of the trees, giggling and shrieking, not too far in, just far enough for it to be scary, for the branch shapes to look like faces and clawed hands, for the wolves to rustle and creep in the greyness you couldn't quite see into, the clotted shifting depths of the place.

But after, lying on your stomach at home on the hearthrug watching telly with the curtains drawn and the dark shut out, it was cosy to think of Packer's End, where you weren't.

After they were twelve or so the witches and wolves went away. Then it was the German plane. And other things too. You didn't know who there might be around, in woods and places. Like stories in the papers. Girl attacked on lonely road.

Police hunt rapist. There was this girl, people at school said, this girl some time back who'd been biking along the field path and these two blokes had come out of Packer's End. They'd had a knife, they'd threatened to carve her up, there wasn't anything she could do, she was at their mercy. People couldn't remember what her name was, exactly, she didn't live round here any more. Two enormous blokes, sort of gypsy types.

She put her sandal back on. She walked through the thicker grass by the hedge and felt it drag at her legs and thought of swimming in warm seas. She put her hand on the top of her head and her hair was hot from the sun, a dry burning cap. One day, this year, next year, sometime, she would go to places like on travel brochures and run into a blue sea. She would fall in love and she would get a good job and she would have one of those new Singers that do zig-zag stitch and make an embroidered silk coat.

One day.

Now, she would go to this old Mrs Rutter's and have a bit of a giggle with Susie and come home for tea and wash her hair. She would walk like this through the silken grass with the wind seething the corn and the secret invisible life of birds beside her in the hedge. She would pick a blue flower and examine its complexity of pattern and petal and wonder what it was called and drop it. She would plunge her face into the powdery plate of an elderflower and smell cat, tom-cat, and sneeze and scrub her nose with the back of her hand. She would hurry through the gate and over the stream because that was a bit too close to Packer's End for comfort and she would . . .

He rose from the plough beyond the hedge.

She screamed.

'Christ!' she said. 'Kerry Stevens, you stupid so-and-so, what d'you want to go and do that for you give me the fright of my life.'

He grinned. 'I seen you coming. Thought I might as well wait.'

Not Susie. Not Liz either. Kerry Stevens from Richmond Way. Kerry Stevens that none of her lot reckoned much on, with his black licked-down hair and slitty eyes. Some people you only have to look at to know they're not up to much.

'Didn't know you were in the Good Neighbours.'

He shrugged. They walked in silence. He took out an Aero bar, broke off a bit, offered it. She said, 'Oh, thanks.' They went chewing towards the cottage where old Mrs Rutter with her wonky leg would be ever so pleased to see them because they were really sweet, lots of the old people. Ever so grateful the old poppets was what Pat said, not that you'd put it quite like that yourself.

'Just give it a push, the door. It sticks, see. That's it.'

She seemed composed of circles, a cottage-loaf of a woman, with a face below which chins collapsed one into another, a creamy smiling pool of a face in which her eyes snapped and darted.

'Tea, my duck?' she said. 'Tea for the both of you? I'll put us a kettle on.'

The room was stuffy. It had a gaudy lino floor with the pattern rubbed away in front of the sink and round the table; the walls were cluttered with old calendars and pictures torn from magazines; there was a smell of cabbage. The alcove by the fireplace was filled with china ornaments: big-eyed flop-eared rabbits and beribboned kittens and flowery milkmaids and a pair of naked chubby children wearing daisy chains.

The woman hauled herself from a sagging armchair. She glittered at them from the stove, manoeuvring cups, propping herself against the draining-board. 'What's your names, then? Sandra and Kerry. Well, you're a pretty girl, Sandra, aren't you. Pretty as they come. There was — let me see, who was it?

— Susie, last week. That's right, Susie.' Her eyes investigated, quick as mice. 'Put your jacket on the back of the door, dear, you won't want to get that messy. Still at school, are you?'

The boy said, 'I'm leaving, July. They're taking me on at the garage, the Blue Star. I been helping out there on and off, before.'

Mrs Rutter's smiles folded into one another. Above them, her eyes examined him. 'Well, I expect that's good steady money if you'd nothing special in mind. Sugar?'

There was a view from the window out over a bedraggled garden with the stumps of spent vegetables and a matted flowerbed and a square of shaggy grass. Beyond, the spinney reached up to the fence, a no-man's-land of willowherb and thistle and small trees, growing thicker and higher into the full density of woodland. Mrs Rutter said, 'Yes, you have a look out, aren't I lucky — right up beside the wood. Lovely it is in the spring, the primroses and that. Mind, there's not as many as there used to be.'

The girl said, 'Have you lived here for a long time?'

'Most of my life, dear. I came here as a young married woman, and that's a long way back, I can tell you. You'll be courting before long yourself, I don't doubt. Like bees round the honeypot, they'll be.'

The girl blushed. She looked at the floor, at her own feet, neat and slim and brown. She touched, secretly, the soft skin of her thigh; she felt her breasts poke up and out at the thin stuff of her top; she licked the inside of her teeth, that had only the one filling, a speck like a pin-head. She wished there was Susie to have a giggle with, not just that Kerry Stevens.

The boy said, 'What'd you like us to do?'

His chin was explosive with acne; at his middle, his jeans yawned from his T-shirt, showing pale chilly flesh. Mrs Rutter said, 'I expect you're a nice strong boy, aren't you? I daresay you'd like to have a go at the grass with the old mower. Sandra can give this room a do, that would be nice, it's as much as I can manage to have a dust of the ornaments just now, I can't get down to the floor.'

When he had gone outside, the girl fetched broom and mop and dustpan from a cupboard under the narrow stair. The cupboard, stacked with yellowing newspapers, smelt of damp and mouse. When she returned, the old woman was back in the armchair, a composite chintzy mass from which cushions oozed and her voice flowed softly on. 'That's it, dear, you just work round, give the corners a brush if you don't mind, that's where the dust settles. Mind your pretty skirt, pull it up a bit, there's only me to see if you're showing a bit of bum. That's ever such a nice style, I expect your mum made it, did she?'

The girl said, 'Actually I did.'

'Well now, fancy! You're a little dressmaker, too, are you? I was good with my needle when I was younger, my eyesight's past it now, of course. I made my own wedding-dress, ivory silk with lace insets. A Vogue pattern it was, with a sweetheart neckline.'

The door opened. Kerry said, 'Where'll I put the clippings?'

'There's the compost heap down the bottom, by the fence. And while you're down there could you get some sticks from the wood for kindling, there's a good lad.'

When he had gone she went on, 'That's a nice boy. It's a pity they put that stuff on their hair these days, sticky-looking. I expect you've got lots of boyfriends, though, haven't you?'

The girl poked in a crack at a clump of fluff. 'I don't really know Kerry that much.'

'Don't you, dear. Well, I expect you get all sorts, in your club thing, the club that Miss Hammond runs.'

'The Good Neighbours. Pat, we call her.'

'She was down here last week. Ever such a nice person. Kind. It's sad she never married.'

The girl said, 'Is that your husband in the photo, Mrs Rutter?'

'That's right, dear. In his uniform. The Ox and Bucks. After he got his stripes. He was a lovely man.'

She sat back on her heels, the dustpan on her lap. The photo was yellowish, in a silver frame. 'Did he ...?'

'Killed in the war, dear. Right at the start. He was in one of the first campaigns, in Belgium, and he never came back.'

The girl saw a man with a tooth-brush moustache, his army cap slicing his forehead. 'That's terrible.'

'Tragic. There was a lot of tragedies in the war. It's nice it won't be like that for you young people nowadays. Touch wood, cross fingers. I like young people, I never had any children, it's been a loss, that, I've got a sympathy with young people.'

The girl emptied the dustpan into the bin outside the back door. Beyond the fence, she could see the bushes thrash and Kerry's head bob among them. She thought, rather him than me, but it's different for boys, for him anyway, he's not a nervy type, it's if you're nervy you get bothered about things like Packer's End.

She was nervy, she knew. Mum always said so.

Mrs Rutter was rummaging in a cupboard by her chair. 'Chocky? I always keep a few chockies by for visitors.' She brought out a flowered tin. 'There. Do you know, I've had this twenty years, all but. Look at the little cornflowers. And the daisies. They're almost real, aren't they?'

'Sweet,' said the girl.

'Take them out and see if what's-'is-name would like one.'

There was a cindery path down the garden, ending at a compost heap where eggshells gleamed among leaves and grass clippings. Rags of plastic fluttered from sticks in a bed of cabbages. The girl picked her way daintily, her toes wincing against the cinders. A place in the country. One day she would have a place in the country, but not like this. Sometime. A little white house peeping over a hill, with a stream at the bottom of a crisp green lawn and an orchard with old apple trees and a brown pony. And she would walk in the long grass in this orchard in a straw hat with these two children, a boy and a girl, children with fair shiny hair like hers, and there'd be this man.

She leaned over the fence and shouted, 'Hey . . .'

'What?'

She brandished the box.

He came up, dumping an armful of sticks. 'What's this for, then?'

'She said. Help yourself.'

He fished among the sweets, his fingers etched with dirt. 'I did a job on your dad's car last week. That blue Escort's his, isn't it?'

'Mm.'

'July, I'll be starting full-time. When old Bill retires. With day-release at the tech.'

She thought of oily workshop floors, of the foetid undersides of cars. She couldn't stand the feel of dirt; if her hands were the least bit grubby she had to go and wash; a rim of grime under her nails could make her shudder. She said, 'I don't know how you can, all that muck.'

He fished for another chocolate. 'Nothing wrong with a bit of dirt. What you going to do, then?'

'Secretarial.'

Men didn't mind so much. At home, her dad did things like unblocking the sink and cleaning the stove; Mum was the same as her, just the feel of grease and stuff made her squirm. They couldn't either of them wear anything that had a stain or a spot.

He said, 'I don't go much on her.'

'Who?'

He waved towards the cottage.

'She's all right. What's wrong with her, then?'

He shrugged. 'I dunno. The way she talks and that.'

'She lost her husband,' said the girl. 'In the war.' She considered him, across the fence, over a chasm. Mum said boys matured later, in many ways.

'There's lots of people done that.'

She looked beyond him, into distances. 'Tragic, actually. Well, I'll go back and get on. She says can you see to her bins when you've got the sticks. She wants them carried down for the dustmen.'

Mrs Rutter watched her come in, glinting from the cushions. 'That's a good girl. Put the tin back in the cupboard, dear.'

'What would you like me to do now?'

'There's my little bit of washing by the sink. Just the personal things to rinse through. That would be ever so kind.'

The girl ran water into the basin. She measured in the soapflakes. She squeezed the pastel nylons, the floating sinuous tights. 'It's a lovely colour, that turquoise.'

'My niece got me that last Christmas. Nightie and a little jacket to go. I was telling you about my wedding dress. The material came from Macy's, eight yards. I cut it on the cross, for the hang. Of course, I had a figure then.' She heaved herself round in the chair. 'You're a lovely shape, Sandra. You take care you stay that way.'

'I can get a spare tyre,' the girl said. 'If I'm not careful.'

Outside, the bin lids rattled.

'I hope he's minding my edging. I've got lobelia planted out along that path.'

'I love blue flowers.'

'You should see the wood in the spring, with the bluebells.

There's a place right far in where you get lots coming up still. I used to go in there picking every year before my leg started playing me up. Jugs and jugs of them, for the scent. Haven't you ever seen them?'

The girl shook her head. She wrung out the clothes, gathered up the damp skein. 'I'll put these on the line, shall I?'

When she returned the boy was bringing in the filled coal-scuttle and a bundle of sticks.

'That's it,' said Mrs Rutter. 'Under the sink, that's where they go. You'll want to have a wash after that, won't you. Put the kettle on, Sandra, and we'll top up the pot.'

The boy ran his hands under the tap. His shirt clung to his shoulderblades, damp with sweat. He looked over the bottles of detergent, the jug of parsley, the handful of flowers tucked into a Coronation mug. He said, 'Is that the wood where there was that German plane came down in the war?'

'Don't start on that,' said the girl. 'It always gives me the willies.'

'What for?'

'Scary.'

The old woman reached forward and prodded the fire. 'Put a bit of coal on for me, there's a good boy. What's to be scared of? It's over and done with, good riddance to bad rubbish.'

'It was there, then?'

'Shut up,' said the girl.

'Were you here?'

'Fill my cup up, dear, would you. I was here. Me and my sister. My sister Dot. She's dead now, two years. Heart. That was before she was married, of course, nineteen forty-two, it was.'

'Did you see it come down?'

She chuckled. 'I saw it come down all right.'

'What was it?' said the boy. 'Messerschmitt?'

'How would I know that, dear? I don't know anything

about aeroplanes. Anyway, it was all smashed up by the time I saw it, you couldn't have told t'other from which.'

The girl's hand hovered, the tea-cup halfway to her mouth. She sipped, put it down. 'You *saw* it? Ooh, I wouldn't have gone anywhere near.'

'It would have been burning,' said the boy. 'It'd have gone up in flames.'

'There weren't any flames; it was just stuck there in the ground, end up, with mess everywhere. Drop more milk, dear, if you don't mind.'

The girl shuddered. 'I s'pose they'd taken the bodies away by then.'

Mrs Rutter picked out a tea-leaf with the tip of the spoon. She drank, patted the corner of her mouth delicately with a tissue. 'No, no, course not. There was no one else seen it come down. We'd heard the engine and you could tell there was trouble, the noise wasn't right, and we looked out and saw it come down smack in the trees. 'Course we hadn't the telephone so there was no ringing the police or the Warden at Clapton. Dot said we should maybe bike to the village but it was a filthy wet night, pouring cats and dogs, and fog too, and we didn't know if it was one of ours or one of theirs, did we? So Dot said better go and have a look first.'

'But either way ...' the boy began.

'We got our wellies on, and Dot had the big lantern, and we went off. It wasn't very far in. We found it quite quick and Dot grabbed hold of me and pointed and we saw one of the wings sticking up with the markings on and we knew it was one of theirs. We cheered, I can tell you.'

The boy stared at her over the rim of the cup, blank-faced.

'Dot said bang goes some more of the bastards, come on let's get back into the warm and we just started back when we heard this noise.'

'Noise?'

'Sort of a moaning.'

'Oh,' cried the girl. 'How awful, weren't they . . .'

'So we got up closer and Dot held the lantern so we could see and there was three of them, two in the front and they were dead, you could see that all right, one of them had his . . .'

The girl grimaced. 'Don't.'

Mrs Rutter's chins shook, the pink and creamy chins. 'Good job you weren't there then, my duck. Not that we were laughing at the time, I can tell you, rain teeming down and a raw November night, and that sight under our noses. It wasn't pretty but I've never been squeamish, nor Dot neither. And then we saw the other one.'

'The other one?' said the boy warily.

'The one at the back. He was trapped, see, the way the plane had broken up. There wasn't any way he could get out.'

The girl stiffened. 'Oh, lor, you mean he . . .'

'He was hurt pretty bad. He was kind of talking to himself. Something about mutter, mutter . . . Dot said he's not going to last long, and a good job too, three of them that'll be. She'd been a VAD so she knew a bit about casualties, see.' Mrs Rutter licked her lips; she looked across at them, her eyes darting. 'Then we went back to the cottage.'

There was silence. The fire gave a heave and a sigh. 'You what?' said the boy.

'Went back inside. It was bucketing down, cats and dogs.'

The boy and girl sat quite still, on the far side of the table.

'That was eighteen months or so after my hubby didn't come back from Belgium.' Her eyes were on the girl; the girl looked away. 'Tit for tat, I said to Dot.'

After a moment she went on. 'Next morning it was still raining and blow me if the bike hadn't got a puncture. I said to Dot I'm not walking to the village in this, and that's flat, and Dot was running a bit of a temp, she had the 'flu or something coming on. I tucked her up warm and when I'd done the chores I went back in the wood, to have another look. He must have been a tough so-and-so, that jerry, he was still mumbling away. It gave me a turn, I can tell you, I'd never imagined he'd last the night. I could see him better, in the daytime; he was bashed up pretty nasty. I'd thought he was an old bloke, too, but he wasn't. He'd have been twentyish, that sort of age.'

The boy's spoon clattered to the floor; he did not move.

'I reckon he may have seen me, not that he was in a state to take much in. He called out something. I thought, oh no, you had this coming to you, mate, there's a war on. You won't know that expression — it was what everybody said in those days. I thought, why should I do anything for you? Nobody did anything for my Bill, did they? I was a widow at thirty-nine. I've been on my own ever since.'

The boy shoved his chair back from the table.

'He must have been a tough bastard, like I said. He was still there that evening, but the next morning he was dead. The weather'd perked up by then and I walked to the village and got a message to the people at Clapton. They were ever so surprised; they didn't know there'd been a jerry plane come down in the area at all. There were lots of people came to take bits for souvenirs, I had a bit myself but it's got mislaid, you tend to mislay things when you get to my age.'

The boy had got up. He glanced down at the girl. 'I'm going,' he said. 'Dunno about you, but I'm going.'

She stared at the lacy cloth on the table, the fluted china cup. 'I'll come too.'

'Eh?' said the old woman. 'You're off, are you? That was nice of you to see to my little jobs for me. Tell what's-'er-name to send someone next week if she can, I like having someone young about the place, once in a while, I've got a sympathy with young people. Here — you're forgetting your pretty jacket, Sandra, what's the hurry? 'Bye then, my ducks, see you close my gate, won't you?'

The boy walked ahead, fast; the girl pattered behind him, sliding on the dry grass. At the gateway into the cornfield he stopped. He said, not looking at her, looking towards the furzy edge of the wood, 'Christ!'

The wood sat there in the afternoon sun. Wind stirred the trees. Birds sang. There were not, the girl realised, wolves or witches or tigers. Nor were there prowling blokes, gypsy-type blokes. And there were not chattering ghostly voices. Somewhere there were some scraps of metal overlooked by people hunting for souvenirs.

The boy said, 'I'm not going near that old bitch again.' He leaned against the gate, clenching his fists on an iron rung; he shook slightly. 'I won't ever forget him, that poor sod.'

She nodded.

'Two bloody nights. Christ!'

And she would hear, she thought, always, for a long time anyway, that voice trickling on, that soft old woman's voice; would see a tin painted with cornflowers, pretty china ornaments.

'It makes you want to throw up,' he said. 'Someone like that.'

She couldn't think of anything to say. He had grown; he had got older and larger. His anger eclipsed his acne, the patches of grease on his jeans, his lardy midriff. You could get people all wrong, she realised with alarm. You could get people wrong and there was a darkness that was not the darkness of tree shadows and murky undergrowth and you could not draw the curtains and keep it out because it was in your head, once known, in your head for ever like lines from a song. One moment you were walking in long grass with the sun on your hair and birds singing and the next you glimpsed darkness, an inescapable darkness. The darkness was out there and it was a part of you and you would never be without it, ever.

She walked behind him, through a world grown unreliable, in which flowers sparkle and birds sing but everything is not as it appears, oh no.

Thinking it over

1 What did you think of Sandra as she was on her way to Mrs Rutter's? And what did you think of Kerry then? Talk about how they are presented in the first part of the story. Pick out the words and phrases the author uses in order to help you to form your opinions of them.

2 a) What was your first impression of Mrs Rutter, when Sandra and Kerry arrived at the cottage and started doing her chores?

b) Did you change your opinion of Mrs Rutter by the end of the story? What do you think of the way she and her sister behaved? Can you understand why she behaved as she did? Do you sympathise with her at all or do you feel there is no excuse for what she did?

3 How do Kerry and Sandra react to Mrs Rutter's story? In what way does it affect them? How are they changed as a result of their visit to Mrs Rutter's?

4 How did you feel at the end of the story? Did you find it a very bleak, depressing story? Were you reassured in any way by how both Kerry and Sandra reacted to Mrs Rutter's story? Write a short statement summing up your feelings about the story, then form groups and discuss what you have written.

5 How easy did you find it to visualise the setting of this story? Talk about the details of Packer's End and Nether Cottage that are included in the story. Imagine what a photograph of the cottage would be like. Either describe the cottage in your own words or draw a picture of it.

6 Talk about the title of the story. 'First impressions' has been suggested as an alternative title. Do you prefer it to the actual title? Say why. Can you suggest any other alternative titles?

Role play

How did you get on?
At the next meeting of the Good Neighbours Club, Miss Hammond asks Kerry or Sandra how they got on at Mrs Rutter's. Act out the conversation that takes place.

I'm not going back there
That night Sandra meets her friend Susie. She tells Susie about what happened at Mrs Rutter's. (Remember that Susie knows Mrs Rutter, because she has been there the previous week.)

How the author tells the story

1 a) The most important part of this story is what Mrs Rutter reveals about herself in the conversation about the plane crash. Study it and pick out the words and phrases the author uses to let us know how Sandra and Kerry are reacting to her story.

b) Write your own story in which a conversation plays a key part. Make it clear, as Penelope Lively does, how your characters are affected by what they learn during the course of the conversation.

2 a) At the end of the story, how does the author let you know what she herself feels about the transformation in Kerry and Sandra as they leave Mrs Rutter's? What signs are there that the author is giving her opinion rather than just narrating?

b) Try describing an incident on a bright sunny day which has a profound effect on the characters concerned and changes them in some way. Write in the third person. Do more than simply narrate the events. Write in such a way that you make your opinion about the incident quite clear.

9: A sunrise on the veld

DORIS LESSING

Every night that winter he said aloud into the dark of the pillow: Half past four! Half past four! till he felt his brain had gripped the words and held them fast. Then he fell asleep at once, as if a shutter had fallen; and lay with his face turned to the clock so that he could see it first thing when he woke.

It was half past four to the minute, every morning. Triumphantly pressing down the alarm-knob of the clock, which the dark half of his mind had outwitted, remaining vigilant all night and counting the hours as he lay relaxed in sleep, he huddled down for a last warm moment under the clothes, playing with the idea of lying abed for this once only. But he played with it for the fun of knowing that it was a weakness he could defeat without effort; just as he set the alarm each night for the delight of the moment when he woke and stretched his limbs, feeling the muscles tighten, and thought: Even my brain — even that! I can control every part of myself.

Luxury of warm rested body, with the arms and legs and fingers waiting like soldiers for a word of command! Joy of knowing that the precious hours were given to sleep voluntarily! — for he had once stayed awake three nights running, to prove that he could, and then worked all day, refusing even to admit that he was tired; and now sleep seemed to him a servant to be commanded and refused.

The boy stretched his frame full-length, touching the wall at his head with his hands, and the bedfoot with his toes; then he sprang out, like a fish leaping from water. And it was cold, cold.

He always dressed rapidly, so as to try and conserve his night-warmth till the sun rose two hours later; but by the time he had on his clothes his hands were numbed and he could scarcely hold his shoes. These he could not put on for fear of waking his parents, who never came to know how early he rose.

As soon as he stepped over the lintel, the flesh of his soles contracted on the chilled earth, and his legs began to ache with cold. It was night: the stars were glittering, the trees standing black and still. He looked for signs of day, for the greying of the edge of a stone, or a lightening in the sky where the sun would rise, but there was nothing yet. Alert as an animal he crept past the dangerous window, standing poised with his hand on the sill for one proudly fastidious moment, looking in at the stuffy blackness of the room where his parents lay.

Feeling for the grass-edge of the path with his toes, he reached inside another window farther along the wall, where his gun had been set in readiness the night before. The steel was icy, and numbed fingers slipped along it, so that he had to hold it in the crook of his arm for safety. Then he tiptoed to the room where the dogs slept, and was fearful that they might have been tempted to go before him; but they were waiting, their haunches crouched in reluctance at the cold, but ears and swinging tails greeting the gun ecstatically. His warning undertone kept them secret and silent till the house was a hundred yards back: then they bolted off into the bush, yelping excitedly. The boy imagined his parents turning in their beds and muttering: Those dogs again! before they were dragged back in sleep; and he smiled scornfully. He always looked back over his shoulder at the house before he passed a wall of trees that shut it from sight. It looked so low and small, crouching there under a tall and brilliant sky. Then he turned his back on it, and on the frowsting sleepers, and forgot them.

He would have to hurry. Before the light grew strong he must be four miles away; and already a tint of green stood in the hollow of a leaf, and the air smelled of morning and the stars were dimming.

He slung the shoes over his shoulder, veld skoen that were crinkled and hard with the dews of a hundred mornings. They would be necessary when the ground became too hot to bear. Now he felt the chilled dust push up between his toes, and he let the muscles of his feet spread and settle into the shapes of the earth; and he thought: I could walk a hundred miles on feet like these! I could walk all day, and never tire!

He was walking swiftly through the dark tunnel of foliage that in daytime was a road. The dogs were invisibly ranging the lower travelways of the bush, and he heard them panting. Sometimes he felt a cold muzzle on his leg before they were off again, scouting for a trail to follow. They were not trained, but free-running companions of the hunt, who often tired of the long stalk before the final shots, and went off on their own pleasure. Soon he could see them, small and wild-looking in a wild strange light, now that the bush stood trembling on the verge of colour, waiting for the sun to paint earth and grass afresh.

The grass stood to his shoulders; and the trees were showering a faint silvery rain. He was soaked; his whole body was clenched in a steady shiver.

Once he bent to the road that was newly scored with animal trails, and regretfully straightened, reminding himself that the pleasure of tracking must wait till another day.

He began to run along the edge of a field, noting jerkily how it was filmed over with fresh spiderweb, so that the long reaches of great black clods seemed netted in glistening grey. He was using the steady lope he had learned by watching the natives, the run that is a dropping of the weight of the body from one foot to the next in a slow balancing movement that never tires, nor shortens the breath; and he felt the blood pulsing down his legs and along his arms, and the exultation and pride of body mounted in him till he was shutting his teeth hard against a violent desire to shout his triumph.

Soon he had left the cultivated part of the farm. Behind him the bush was low and black. In front was a long vlei, acres of long pale grass that sent back a hollowing gleam of light to a satiny sky. Near him thick swathes of grass were bent with the weight of water, and diamond drops sparkled on each frond.

The first bird woke at his feet and at once a flock of them sprang into the air calling shrilly that day had come; and suddenly behind him, the bush woke into song, and he could hear the guinea-fowl calling far ahead of him. That meant they would not be sailing down from their trees into thick grass, and it was for them he had come: he was too late. But he did not mind. He forgot he had come to shoot. He set his legs wide, and balanced from foot to foot, and swung his gun up and down in both hands horizontally, in a kind of improvised exercise, and let his head sink back till it was pillowed in his neck muscles, and watched how above him small rosy clouds floated in a lake of gold.

Suddenly it all rose in him: it was unbearable. He leapt up into the air, shouting and yelling wild, unrecognisable noises. Then he began to run, not carefully, as he had before, but madly, like a wild thing. He was clean crazy, yelling mad with the joy of living and a superfluity of youth. He rushed down the vlei under a tumult of crimson and gold, while all the birds of the world sang about him. He ran in great leaping strides, and shouted as he ran, feeling his body rise into the crisp rushing air and fall back surely on to sure feet; and thought briefly, not believing that such a thing could happen to him, that he could break his ankle any moment, in this thick tangled grass. He cleared bushes like a duiker, leaped over rocks; and finally came to a dead stop at a place where the ground fell abruptly away below him to the river. It had been a two-mile-long dash through waist-high growth, and he was breathing hoarsely and could no longer sing. But he poised on a rock and looked down at stretches of water that gleamed through stooping trees, and thought suddenly, I am fifteen! Fifteen! The words came new to him; so that he kept repeating them wonderingly, with swelling excitement; and he felt the years of his life with his hands, as if he were counting marbles, each one hard and separate and compact, each one a wonderful shining thing. That was what he was: fifteen years of this rich soil, and this slow-moving water, and air that smelt like a challenge whether it was warm and sultry at noon, or as brisk as cold water, like it was now.

There was nothing he couldn't do, nothing! A vision came to him, as he stood there, like when a child hears the word 'eternity' and tries to understand it, and time takes possession of the mind. He felt his life ahead of him as a great and wonderful thing, something that was his; and he said aloud, with the blood rising to his head: All the great men of the world have been as I am now, and there is nothing I can't become, nothing I can't do; there is no country in the world I cannot make part of myself, if I choose. I contain the world. I can make of it what I want. If I choose, I can change everything that is going to happen: it depends on me, and what I decide now.

The urgency, and the truth and the courage of what his voice was saying exulted him so that he began to sing again, at the top of his voice, and the sound went echoing down the river gorge. He stopped for the echo, and sang again: stopped and shouted. That was what he was!—he sang, if he chose; and the world had to answer him.

And for minutes he stood there, shouting and singing and waiting for the lovely eddying sound of the echo; so that his own new strong thoughts came back and washed round his head, as if someone were answering him and encouraging him: till the gorge was full of soft voices clashing back and forth from rock to rock over the river. And then it seemed as if there was a new voice. He listened, puzzled, for it was not his own. Soon he was leaning forward, all his nerves alert, quite still: somewhere close to him there was a noise that was no joyful bird, nor tinkle of falling water, nor ponderous movement of cattle.

There it was again. In the deep morning hush that held his future and his past, was a sound of pain, and repeated over and over: it was a kind of shortened scream, as if someone, something, had no breath to scream. He came to himself, looked about him, and called for the dogs. They did not appear: they had gone off on their own business, and he was alone. Now he was clean sober, all the madness gone. His heart beating fast, because of that frightened screaming, he stepped carefully off the rock and went towards a belt of trees. He was moving cautiously, for not so long ago he had seen a leopard in just this spot.

At the end of the trees he stopped and peered, holding his gun ready; he advanced, looking steadily about him, his eyes narrowed. Then, all at once, in the middle of a step, he faltered, and his face was puzzled. He shook his head impatiently, as if he doubted his own sight.

There, between two trees, against a background of gaunt black rocks, was a figure from a dream, a strange beast that was horned and drunken-legged, but like something he had never even imagined. It seemed to be ragged. It looked like a small buck that had black ragged tufts of fur standing up irregularly all over it, with patches of raw flesh beneath ... but the patches of rawness were disappearing under moving black and came again elsewhere; and all the time the creature screamed, in small gasping screams, and leaped drunkenly from side to side, as if it were blind.

Then the boy understood: it *was* a buck. He ran closer, and again stood still, stopped by a new fear. Around him the grass was whispering and alive. He looked wildly about, and then down. The ground was black with ants, great energetic ants that took no notice of him, but hurried and scurried towards the fighting shape, like glistening black water flowing through the grass.

And, as he drew in his breath and pity and terror seized him, the beast fell and the screaming stopped. Now he could hear nothing but one bird singing, and the sound of the rustling, whispering ants.

He peered over at the writhing blackness that jerked convulsively with the jerking nerves. It grew quieter. There were small twitches from the mass that still looked vaguely like the shape of a small animal.

It came into his mind that he should shoot it and end its pain; and he raised the gun. Then he lowered it again. The buck could no longer feel; its fighting was a mechanical protest of the nerves. But it was not that which made him put down the gun. It was a swelling feeling of rage and misery and protest that expressed itself in the thought: If I had not come it would have died like this: so why should I interfere? All over the bush things like this happen; they happen all the time; this is how life goes on, by living things dying in anguish. He gripped the gun between his knees and felt in his own limbs the myriad swarming pain of the twitching animal that could no longer feel, and set his teeth, and said over and over again under his breath: I can't stop it. I can't stop it. There is nothing I can do.

He was glad the buck was unconscious and had gone past suffering so that he did not have to make a decision to kill it even when he was feeling with his whole body: this is what happens, this is how things work.

It was right — that was what he was feeling. *It was right and nothing could alter it.*

The knowledge of fatality, of what has to be, had gripped him and for the first time in his life; and he was left unable to make any movement of brain or body, except to say: 'Yes, yes. That is what living is.' It had entered his flesh and his bones and grown into the farthest corners of his brain and would never leave him. And at that moment he could not have performed the smallest action of mercy, knowing as he did, having lived on it all his life, the vast unalterable cruel veld, where at any moment one might stumble over a skull or crush the skeleton of some small creature.

Suffering, sick, and angry, but also grimly satisfied with his new stoicism, he stood there leaning on his rifle, and watched the seething black mound grow smaller. At his feet, now, were ants trickling back with pink fragments in their mouths, and there was a fresh acid smell in his nostrils. He sternly controlled the uselessly convulsing muscles of his empty stomach, and reminded himself the ants must eat too! At the same time he found that the tears were streaming down his face, and his clothes were soaked with the sweat of that other creature's pain.

The shape had grown small. Now it looked like nothing recognizable. He did not know how long it was before he saw the blackness thin, and bits of white showed through, shining in the sun — yes, there was the sun, just up, glowing over the rocks. Why, the whole thing could not have taken longer than a few minutes.

He began to swear, as if the shortness of the time was in itself unbearable, using the words he had heard his father say. He strode forward, crushing ants with each step, and brushing them off his clothes, till he stood above the skeleton, which lay sprawled under a small bush. It was clean-picked. It might have been lying there years, save that on the white bones were pink fragments of gristle. About the bones ants were ebbing away, their pincers full of meat.

The boy looked at them, big black ugly insects. A few were standing and gazing up at him with small glittering eyes.

'Go away!' he said to the ants, very coldly. 'I am not for you — not just yet, at any rate. Go away.' And he fancied that the ants turned and went away.

He bent over the bones and touched the sockets in the skull; that was where the eyes were, he thought incredulously, remembering the liquid dark eyes of a buck. And then he bent the slim foreleg bone, swinging it horizontally in his palm.

That morning, perhaps an hour ago, this small creature had been stepping proud and free through the bush, feeling the chill on its hide even as he himself had done, exhilarated by it. Proudly stepping the earth, tossing its horns, frisking a pretty white tail, it had sniffed the cold morning air. Walking like kings and conquerors it had moved through this free-held bush, where each blade of grass grew for it alone, and where the river ran pure sparkling water for its slaking.

And then — what had happened? Such a swift surefooted thing could surely not be trapped by a swarm of ants?

The boy bent curiously to the skeleton. Then he saw that the back leg that lay uppermost and strained out in the tension of death was snapped midway in the thigh, so that broken bones jutted over each other uselessly. So that was it! Limping into the ant-masses it could not escape, once it had sensed the danger. Yes, but how had the leg been broken? Had it fallen, perhaps? Impossible, a buck was too light and graceful. Had some jealous rival horned it?

What could possibly have happened? Perhaps some Africans had thrown stones at it, as they do, trying to kill it for meat, and had broken its leg. Yes, that must be it.

Even as he imagined the crowd of running, shouting natives, and the flying stones, and the leaping buck, another picture came into his mind. He saw himself, on any one of these bright ringing mornings, drunk with excitement, taking a snap shot at some half-seen buck. He saw himself with the gun lowered, wondering whether he had missed or not; and thinking at last that it was late, and he wanted his breakfast, and it was not worthwhile to track miles after an animal that would very likely get away from him in any case.

For a moment he would not face it. He was a small boy again, kicking sulkily at the skeleton, hanging his head, refusing to accept the responsibility.

Then he straightened up, and looked down at the bones with an odd expression of dismay, all the anger gone out of him. His mind went quite empty: all around him he could see trickles of ants disappearing into the grass. The whispering noise was faint and dry, like the rustling of a cast snakeskin.

At last he picked up his gun and walked homewards. He was telling himself half defiantly that he wanted his breakfast. He was telling himself that it was getting very hot, much too hot to be out roaming the bush.

Really, he was tired. He walked heavily, not looking where he put his feet. When he came within sight of his home he stopped, knitting his brows. There was something he had to think out. The death of that small animal was a thing that concerned him, and he was by no means finished with it. It lay at the back of his mind uncomfortably.

Soon, the very next morning, he would get clear of everybody and go to the bush and think about it.

Thinking it over

1 The events of this story take place over a relatively short period of time, during which the boy experiences a sharp change of mood. Where are the boy's (a) highest, (b) lowest moment? And where are the story's highest tension and turning point? Draw a graph. Plot these points on the graph, so that you can see how the story is constructed.

2 How easy did you find it to identify with the boy? What sort of person is he? What do you learn from the story about his background and his attitudes? If your background is very different from his, are you able to understand what he thinks and feels and why?

3 Talk about the ending of the story. Why do you think the author chose to end the story at the point she did? Why doesn't she go on to describe the boy's thoughts the next morning? Did you find it a satisfactory ending? Give your reasons.

4 What do you learn about the countryside in which this story is set? Pick out the details in the descriptions which enable you to visualise the scene and which show that the author is describing a land she knows well.

5 This is another example of a female writer writing about a teenage boy. Would you call this a 'masculine' story? Could the central character just as easily have been a teenage girl?

Role play

Imagine that the boy has a close friend. He attempts to tell the friend about his experience that morning and what he has learned from it.

How the author tells the story

1 a) What parallels do you see between this story and Penelope Lively's 'The Darkness Out There'? Are the authors determined to dash our optimism? Or are they telling us something more?

   b) See if you can write a story of your own which focuses on a significant moment in a teenager's life and describes an experience, as a result of which the central character grows up in some way.

2 a) There is almost no dialogue in this story, only description. But what do you notice about the place where the one spoken phrase breaks into the story? Is it put there for a reason?

b) Try writing a purely descriptive story of your own. You will need to think carefully where to break your narrative into paragraphs. As you draft your story, refer back to Doris Lessing's story to see how she has used paragraphs to break up the narrative.

10: Watermelon moon

BORDEN DEAL

When I think of the summer I was sixteen, a lot of things come crowding in to be thought about. We had moved just the year before, and sixteen is still young enough for the bunch one goes with to make a difference. I had a bunch, all right, but they weren't sure of me yet. I didn't know why. Maybe because I'd lived in town, and my father still worked there instead of farming, like the other fathers did. The boys I knew, even Freddy Gray and J.D., still kept a small distance between us.

Then there was Willadean Wills. I hadn't been much interested in girls before. But I had to admit to myself that I was interested in Willadean. She was my age, nearly as tall as I, and up till the year before, Freddy Gray told me, she had been good at playing their games. But she didn't play games this year. She was tall and slender, and Freddy Gray and J.D. and I had several discussions about the way she walked. I maintained she was putting it on, but J.D. claimed she couldn't help it. Freddy Gray remarked that she hadn't walked that way last year. He said she'd walked like any other human being. So then I said, put on or not, I liked the way she walked, and then there was a large silence.

It wasn't a comfortable silence, because of Mr Wills, Willadean's father. We were all afraid of Mr Wills.

Mr Wills was a big man. He had bright, fierce eyes under heavy brows and, when he looked down at you, you just withered. The idea of having him directly and immediately angry at one of us was enough to shrivel the soul. All that summer Willadean walked up and down the high road or sat in their front garden in a rocking chair, her dress flared out around her, and not one of us dared do more than say good morning to her.

Mr Wills was the best farmer in the community. My father said he could drive a stick into the ground and grow a tree out of it. But it wasn't an easy thing with him; Mr Wills fought the earth when he worked it. When he ploughed his fields, you could hear him yelling for a mile. It was as though he dared the earth not to yield him its sustenance.

Above all, Mr Wills could raise watermelons. Now, watermelons are curious things. Some men can send off for the best watermelon seed, they can plant it in the best ground they own, they can hoe it and tend it with the greatest of care, and they can't raise a melon bigger than your two fists. Other men, like Mr Wills, can throw seed on the ground, scuff dirt over it, walk off and leave it and have a crop of the prettiest, biggest melons you ever saw.

Mr Wills always planted the little field directly behind his barn with watermelons. It ran from the barn to the creek, a good piece of land with just the right sandy soil for melon raising. And it seemed as though the melons just bulged up out of the ground for him.

But they were Mr Wills' melons; he didn't have any idea of sharing them with the boys of the neighbourhood. He was fiercer about his melons than anything else; if you just happened to walk close to his melon patch, you'd see Mr Wills standing and watching you with a glower on his face. And likely as not he'd have his gun under his arm.

Everybody expected to lose a certain quantity of their watermelons to terrapins and a certain quantity to boys. It wasn't considered stealing to sneak into a man's melon patch and judiciously borrow a sample of his crop. You might get a load of salt in the seat of your shorts if you were seen, but that was part of the game. You'd be looked down on only if you got malicious and stamped a lot of melons into the ground while you were about it. But Mr Wills didn't think that way.

That summer I was sixteen Mr Wills raised the greatest watermelon ever seen in that part of the country. It grew in the very middle of his patch, three times as big as any melon anybody had ever seen. Men came from miles around to look at it. Mr Wills wouldn't let them go into the melon patch. They had to stand around the edge.

Just like all other daredevil boys in that part of the world, Freddy Gray and J.D. and I had talked idly about stealing that giant watermelon. But we all knew that it was just talk. Not only were we afraid of Mr Wills and his rages but we knew that Mr Wills sat in the hayloft window of his barn every night with his shotgun, guarding the melon. It was his seed melon. He meant to plant next year's crop out of that great one and maybe grow a whole field of them. Mr Wills was in a frenzy of fear that somebody would steal it. Why, he would rather you stole Willadean than his melon. At least, he didn't guard Willadean with his shotgun.

Every night I could sit on our front porch and see Mr Wills sitting up there in the window of his hayloft, looking fiercely out over his melon patch. I'd sit there by the hour and watch him, the shotgun cradled in his arm, and feel the tremors of fear and excitement chasing up and down my spine.

'Look at him,' my father would say. 'Scared to death somebody will steal his seed melon. Nobody would steal a man's seed melon.'

'He ought to be in the house taking care of that wife of his,' my mother would say tartly. 'She's been poorly all year.'

You hardly ever saw Mrs Wills. She was a wraith of a woman, pale as a butter bean. Sometimes she would sit for an hour or two in their garden in the cool of the day. They didn't visit back and forth with anybody though.

'There's Willadean,' my father would say mildly.

My mother would make a funny kind of sound that meant disgust. 'He cares more about that seed melon than about his wife,' she'd say. 'I wish somebody would steal it. Maybe then—'

'Helen,' my father would say, chiding, 'you shouldn't even think of such a thing.'

About the time the great watermelon was due to become ripe, there was a night of a full moon. J.D. and Freddy Gray and I had decided we'd go swimming in the creek, so I left the house when the moon rose and went to meet them.

The moon floated up into the sky, making everything almost as bright as day, but at the same time softer and gentler than ever daylight could be. It was the kind of night when you feel as though you can do anything in the world — even boldly ask Willadean Wills for a date. On a night like that, you couldn't help but feel that she'd gladly accept.

'Boy, what a moon!' J.D. said when I met them.

'Wouldn't you like to take old Willadean out on a night like this?' Freddy Gray said.

We scoffed at him, but secretly in our hearts we knew how he felt. We were getting old enough to think that that sort of thing might be a lot more fun than going swimming in the moonlight.

As I said before I was one of their bunch. J.D. and Freddy Gray were my good friends. But because I was still new, there were certain things and certain feelings where I was left out. This was one of them; they were afraid, because I was more of a stranger to Willadean, that she might like the idea of dating me better than she did either of them. This was all way down under the surface, because none of us had admitted to ourselves that we wanted to be Willadean's boyfriend. But far down though it was, I could feel it, and they could feel it.

'I wish I had a newspaper,' I said then. 'I'll bet you could read it in this moonlight.'

We had reached the swimming hole in the creek, and we began shucking off our clothes. We were all excited by the moonlight, yelling at one another and rushing to be first into the water. Freddy Gray made it first, J.D. and I catapulting in right behind him. The water was cold, and the shock of it struck a chill into us. But we got rid of it by a brisk water fight and then we were all right.

We climbed out finally, to rest, and sat on the bank. That big old moon sailed serenely overhead, climbing higher into the sky, and we lay on our backs to look up at it.

'Old Man Wills won't have to worry about anybody stealing his melon tonight, anyway,' Freddy Gray said. 'Nobody would dare try it, bright as day like it is.'

'He's not taking any chances,' J.D. said. 'I saw him sitting up in that hayloft when I came by, his shotgun loaded with buckshot. That melon is as safe as it would be in the bank.'

'Shucks,' I said in a scoffing voice, 'he ain't got buckshot in that gun. He's just got a load of salt, like anybody else guarding a watermelon patch.'

Freddy Gray sat upright, looking at me. 'Don't kid yourself, son,' he said loftily. 'He told my daddy that he had it loaded with double-ought buckshot.'

'Why,' I said, 'that would kill a man.'

'That's what he's got in mind,' Freddy Gray said, 'if anybody goes after that seed melon.'

It disturbed me more than it should have. After all, I'd never had it in mind to try for the melon, had I?

'I don't believe it,' I said flatly. 'He wouldn't kill anybody over a watermelon. Even a seed melon like that one.'

'Old Man Wills would,' J.D. said.

Freddy Gray was still watching me. 'What's got you into such a tizzy?' he said. 'You weren't planning on going after that melon yourself?'

'Well, yes,' I said. 'As a matter of fact I was.'

There was a moment of respectful silence. Even from me. I hadn't known I was going to say those words. To this day I don't know why I said them. It was all mixed up with Willadean and the rumour of Mr Wills having his gun loaded with double-ought buckshot and the boys still thinking of me as an outsider. It surged up out of me — not the idea of making my name for years to come by such a deed, but the feeling that there was a rightness in defying the world and Mr Wills.

Mixed up with it all there came into my mouth the taste of watermelon. I could taste the sweet red juices oozing over my tongue, feel the delicate threaded redness of the heart as I squeezed the juices out of it.

I stood up. 'As a matter of fact,' I said, 'I'm going after it right now.'

'Wait a minute,' J.D. said in alarm. 'You can't do it on a moonlight night like this. It's two hundred yards from the creek bank to that melon. He'll see you for sure.'

'Wait until a dark night,' Freddy Gray said. 'Wait until—'

'Anybody could steal it on a dark night,' I said scornfully. 'I'm going to take it right out from under his nose. Tonight.'

I began putting on my clothes. My heart was thudding in my chest. I didn't taste watermelon any more; I tasted fear. But it was too late to stop now. Besides, I didn't want to stop.

We dressed silently, and I led the way up the creek bank. We came opposite the watermelon field and ducked down the bank. We pushed through the willows on the other side and looked towards the barn. We could see Mr Wills very plainly. The gun was cradled in his arms, glinting from the moonlight.

'You'll never make it,' J.D. said in a quiet, fateful voice. 'He'll see you before you're six steps away from the creek.'

'You don't think I mean to walk, do you?' I said.

I pushed myself out away from them, on my belly in the grass that grew up around the watermelon hills. I was absolutely flat, closer to the earth than I thought it was possible to get. I looked back once, to see their white faces watching me out of the willows.

I went on, stopping once in a while to look cautiously up towards the barn. He was still there, still quiet. I met a terrapin taking a bite out of a small melon. Terrapins love watermelon, better than boys do. I touched him on the shell and whispered, 'Hullo, brother,' but he didn't acknowledge my greeting. He just drew into his shell. I went on, wishing I was equipped like a terrapin for the job outside as well as inside.

It seemed to take for ever to reach the great melon in the middle of the field. With every move, I expected Mr Wills to see me. Fortunately the grass was high enough to cover me. At last the melon loomed up before me, deep green in the moonlight, and I gasped at the size of it. I'd never seen it so close.

I lay still for a moment, panting. I didn't have the faintest idea how to get it out of the field. Even if I'd stood up, I couldn't have lifted it by myself. A melon is the slipperiest, most cumbersome object in the world. And this was the largest I'd ever seen. It was not a long melon, but a fat round one. Besides, I didn't dare stand up ...

For minutes I didn't move. I lay there, my nostrils breathing up the smell of the earth and the musty smell of the watermelon vines, and I wondered why I was out here in the middle of all that moonlight on such a venture. There was more to it than just bravado. I was proving something to myself — and to Mr Wills and Willadean.

I thought of a tempting way out then. I would carve my name into the deep greenness of the melon. Mr Wills would see it the next morning when he inspected the melon, and he would know that I could have stolen it if I'd wanted to. But no — crawling to the melon wasn't the same thing as actually taking it.

I reached one hand around the melon and found the stem. I broke the tough stem off close against the smooth roundness, and I was committed. I looked towards the barn again. All quiet.

I saw Mr Wills stretch and yawn, and his teeth glistened; the moon was that bright and I was that close.

I struggled around behind the melon and shoved at it. It rolled over sluggishly, and I pushed it again. It was hard work, pushing it down the trough that my body had made through the grass. Dust rose up around me, and I wanted to sneeze. My spine was crawling with the expectation of a shot. Surely he'd see that the melon was gone out of its accustomed space.

It took about a hundred years to push that melon out of the

field. I say that advisedly, because I felt that much older when I finally reached the edge. With the last of my strength I shoved it into the willows and collapsed. I was lying at the edge of the field.

'Come on,' Freddy Gray said, his voice pleading. 'He's —'

I couldn't move. I turned my head. Mr Wills was standing up to stretch and yawn to his content, and then he sat down again. By then I was rested enough to move again. I snaked into the willows, and they grabbed me.

'You did it!' they said. 'By golly, you did it!'

There was no time to bask in their admiration and respect.

'Let's get it on out of here,' I said. 'We're not safe yet.'

We struggled the melon across the creek and up the bank. We started towards the swimming hole. It took all three of us to carry it, and it was hard to get a grip. J.D. and Freddy Gray carried the ends, while I walked behind the melon, grasping the middle. We stumbled and thrashed in our hurry, and we nearly dropped it three or four times. It was the most difficult object I'd ever tried to carry in my life.

At last we reached the swimming hole and sank down, panting. But not for long; the excitement was too strong in us. Freddy Gray reached out a hand and patted the great melon.

'By golly,' he said, 'there it is. All ours.'

'Let's bust it and eat it before somebody comes,' J.D. said.

'Wait a minute,' I said. 'This isn't just any old melon. This is old man Wills' seed melon, and it deserves more respect than to be busted open with a fist. I'm going to cut it.'

I took out my pocketknife and looked at it dubiously. It was small, and the melon was big. We really needed a butcher's knife. But when the little knife penetrated the thick green rind, the melon split of itself perfectly down the middle. There was a ragged, silken, tearing sound, and it lay open before us.

The heart meat, glistening with sweet moisture, was grained with white sugar specks. I tugged at it with two fingers, and a great chunk of the meat came free. I put it into my mouth, closing my eyes. The melon was still warm from the day's sun. Just as in my anticipation, I felt the juice trickle into my throat, sweet and seizing. I had never tasted watermelon so delicious.

The two boys were watching me savour the first bite. I opened my eyes. 'Dive in,' I said graciously. 'Help yourselves.'

We gorged ourselves until we were heavy. Even then, we had only eaten the heart meat, leaving untouched more than we had consumed. We gazed with sated eyes at the leftover melon, still good meat peopled with a multitude of black seeds.

'What are we going to do with it?' I said.

'There's nothing we can do,' J.D. said. 'I can just see us taking a piece of this melon home for the folks.'

'It's eat it or leave it,' Freddy Gray said.

We were depressed suddenly. It was such a waste, after all the struggle and the danger, that we could not eat every bite. I stood up, not looking at the two boys, not looking at the melon.

'Well,' I said. 'I guess I'd better get home.'

'But what about this?' J.D. said insistently, motioning towards the melon.

I kicked half the melon, splitting it in three parts. I stamped one of the chunks under my foot. Then I set methodically to work, destroying the rest of the melon. The boys watched me silently until I picked up a chunk of rind and threw it at them. Then they swept into the destruction also, and we were laughing again. When we stopped, only the battered rinds were left, the meat muddied on the ground, the seed scattered.

We stood silent, looking at one another. 'There was nothing else to do,' I said, and they nodded solemnly.

But the depression went with us towards home, and when we parted we did so with sober voices and gestures. I did not feel triumph or victory as I had expected, though I knew that tonight's action had brought me closer to my friends than I had ever been before.

'Where have you been?' my father asked as I stepped up on the porch. He was sitting in his rocker.

'Swimming,' I said.

I looked towards Mr Wills' barn. The moon was still high and bright, but I could not see him. My breath caught in my throat when I saw him in the field, walking towards the middle. I stood stiffly, watching him. He reached the place where the melon should have been. I saw him hesitate, looking around, then he bent, and I knew he was looking at the depression in the earth where the melon had lain. He straightened; a great strangled cry tearing out of his throat. It chilled me deep down and all the way through, like the cry of a wild animal.

My father jerked himself our of the chair, startled by the sound. He turned in time to see Mr Wills lift the shotgun over his head and hurl it from him, his voice crying out again in a terrible, surging yell of pain and anger.

'Lord, what's the matter?' my father said.

Mr Wills was tearing up and down the melon patch, and I was puzzled by his actions. Then I saw; he was destroying every melon in the patch. He was breaking them open with his feet, silent now, concentrating on his frantic destruction. I was horrified by the awful sight, and my stomach moved sickly.

My father stood for a moment watching him, then he jumped off the porch and ran towards Mr Wills. I followed him. I saw Mrs Wills and Willadean huddled together in the kitchen doorway. My father ran into the melon patch and caught Mr Wills by the arm.

'What's come over you?' he said. 'What's the matter, man?'

Mr Wills struck his grip away. 'They've stolen my seed melon,' he yelled. 'They took it right out from under me.'

My father grabbed him with both arms. He was a brave man, for he was smaller than Mr Wills, and Mr Wills looked insane with anger, his teeth gripped over his lower lip, his eyes gleaming furiously. Mr Wills shoved my father away, striking at him with his fist. My father went down into the dirt. Mr Wills didn't seem to notice. He went back to his task of destruction, raging up and down the field, stamping on melons large and small.

My father got up and began to chase him. But he didn't have a chance. Every time he got close, Mr Wills would sweep his great arm and knock him away again. At last Mr Wills stopped of his own accord. He was standing on the place where the great melon had grown. His chest was heaving with great sobs of breath. He gazed about him at the destruction he had wrought, but I don't think that he saw it.

'They stole my seed melon,' he said. His voice was quieter now than I had ever heard it. I had not believed such quietness was in him. 'They got it away, and now it's gone.'

I saw that tears stood on his cheeks, and I couldn't look at him any more. I'd never seen a grown man cry, crying in such strength.

'I had two plans for that melon,' he told my father. 'Mrs Wills has been poorly all the spring, and she dearly loves the taste of melon. It was her melon for eating, and my melon for planting. She would eat the meat, and next spring I would plant the seeds for the greatest melon crop in the world. Every day she would ask me if the great seed melon was ready yet.'

I looked towards the house. I saw the two women, the mother and the daughter, standing there. I couldn't bear any more. I fled out of the field towards the sanctuary of my house.

I ran past my mother, standing on the porch, and went into my room ...

I didn't sleep that night. I heard my father come in, heard the low-voiced conversation with my mother, heard them go to bed. I lay wide-eyed and watched the moon through the window as it slid slowly down the sky and at last brought a welcome darkness into the world.

I don't know all the things I thought that night. Mostly it was about the terrible thing I had committed so lightly, out of pride and out of being sixteen years old and out of wanting to challenge the older man, the man with the beautiful daughter.

That was the worst of all, that I had done it so lightly, with so little thought of its meaning. In that part of the world and at that time, watermelon-stealing was not a crime. It was tolerated, laughed about. The men told great tales of their own watermelon-stealing days, how they'd been set on by dogs and peppered with salt-loaded shotgun shells. Watermelon-raiding was a game, a ritual of defiance and rebellion by young males. I could remember my own father saying, 'No melon tastes as sweet as a stolen one,' and my mother laughing and agreeing.

But stealing this great seed melon from a man like Mr Wills lay outside the safe magic of the tacit understanding between man and boy. And I knew that it was up to me, at whatever risk, to repair as well as I could the damage I had done.

When it was almost light I rose from my bed and went out into the fresh world. It would be hot later on; but now the air was dew-cool and fragrant. I had found a paper bag in the kitchen, and I carried it in my hand as I walked towards the swimming hole. I stopped there, looking down at the wanton waste we had made of the part of the melon we had not been able to eat. It looked as though Mr Wills had been stamping here too.

I knelt down on the ground, opened the paper bag and

began picking up the black seeds. They were scattered thickly, still stringy with watermelon pulp, and soon my hands were greasy with them. I kept on doggedly, searching out every seed I could find, until at the end I had to crawl over the ground seeking for the last ones.

They nearly filled the paper bag. I went back to the house. By the time I reached it, the sun and my father had risen. He was standing on the porch.

'What happened to you last night?' he said. 'Did you get so frightened you had to run home? It was frightening to watch him, I'll admit that.'

'Father,' I said, 'I've got to go and talk to Mr Wills. Right now. I wish you would come with me.'

He stopped, watching me. 'What's the matter?' he said. 'Did you steal that seed melon of his?'

'Will you come with me?' I said.

His face was dark and thoughtful. 'Why do you want me?'

'Because I'm afraid he'll shoot me,' I said. My voice didn't tremble much, but I couldn't keep it all out.

'Then why are you going?' he said.

'Because I've got to,' I said.

My father watched me for a moment. 'Yes,' he said quietly, 'I guess you have.' He came down the steps and stood beside me. 'I'll go with you,' he said.

We walked the short distance between our house and his. Though it was so near, I had never been in his garden before. I felt my legs trembling as I went up the brick walk and stood at the bottom of the steps, the paper bag in my hand. I knocked and Willadean came to the screen door.

I did not look at her. 'I want to talk to your father.'

She stared at me for a moment, then she disappeared. In a moment Mr Wills appeared in the doorway. His face was marked by the night, his cheeks sunken, his mouth bitten in.

He stared at me absent-mindedly, as though I were only a speck in his thinking.

'What do you want, boy?' he said.

I felt my teeth grit against the words I had to say. I held out the paper bag towards him.

'Mr Wills,' I said, 'here's the seeds from your seed melon. That's all I could bring back.'

I could feel my father standing quietly behind me. Willadean was standing in the doorway, watching. I couldn't take my eyes away from Mr Wills' face.

'Did you steal it?' he said.

'Yes, sir,' I said.

He advanced to the edge of the porch. The shotgun was standing near the door, and I expected him to reach for it. Instead he came towards me, a great powerful man, and leaned down to me.

'Why did you steal it?' he said.

'I don't know,' I said.

'Didn't you know it was my seed melon?'

'Yes, sir,' I said. 'I knew it.'

He straightened up again and his eyes were beginning to gleam. I wanted to run, but I couldn't move.

'And my sick wife hungered for the taste of that melon,' he said, 'Not for herself, like I thought. But to invite the whole neighbourhood in for a slice of it. She knew I wouldn't ever think of anything like that myself. She hungered for that.'

I hung my head. 'I'm sorry,' I said.

He stopped still then, watching me, 'So you brought me the seeds,' he said softly. 'That's not much, boy.'

I lifted my head. 'It was all I could think to do,' I said. 'The melon is gone. But the seeds are next year. That's why I brought them to you.'

'But you ruined this year,' he said.

'Yes, sir,' I said. 'I ruined this year.'

I couldn't look at him any more. I looked at Willadean standing behind him. Her eyes were a puzzle, watching me, and I couldn't tell what she was thinking or feeling.

'I'm about as ashamed of myself last night as you are of yourself,' Mr Wills said. He frowned at me with his heavy brows. 'You ruined one half of it, and I ruined the other. We're both to blame, boy. Both to blame.'

It seemed there ought to be something more for me to say. I searched for it in my mind and discovered only the thought that I had found this morning in the grey light of dawn.

'The seeds are next year,' I said. I looked at him humbly. 'I'll help you plant them, Mr Wills. I'll work very hard.'

Mr Wills looked at my father for the first time. There was a small hard smile on his face, and his eyes didn't look as fierce as they had before.

'A man with a big farm like mine needs a son,' he said. 'But Willadean here was all the good Lord saw fit to give me. Sam, I do wish I had a boy like that.'

He came close to me then, put his hand on my shoulder. 'We can't do anything about this year,' he said. 'But we'll grow next year, won't we? We'll grow it together.'

'Yes, sir,' I said.

I looked past him at Willadean, and her eyes were smiling too. I felt my heart give a great thump in my chest.

'And you don't have to offer the biggest melon in the world to get folks to come visiting,' I blurted. 'Why, I'll sit on the porch with Willadean any time.'

Mr Wills and my father burst out laughing. Willadean was blushing red in the face. But somehow she didn't look mad with me.

Flustered, I began to beat a retreat towards the gate. Then I stopped, looking back at Mr Wills. I couldn't leave yet.

'Can I ask you one thing, Mr Wills?' I said.

He stopped laughing, and there was no fierceness in his voice. 'Anything you want to, boy,' he said.

'Well, I just wanted to know,' I said. 'Was there double-ought buckshot in that gun?'

He reached round and picked up the gun. He unbreeched it and took out a shell. He broken the shell in his strong fingers, and poured the white salt out into his palm.

'You see?' he said.

'Yes, sir,' I said, taking a deep breath. 'I see.'

I went on then — and the next year started that very day.

Thinking it over

1 Study the introductory section and talk about how the author uses it to set the scene for the rest of the story. What do you learn from it about (a) the boy and his friends, (b) Willadean Wills, (c) watermelon-stealing, (d) Mr Wills and his watermelons?

2 Discuss what happens in the story and why the boy behaved as he did. Why did he decide to steal the melon? How did he feel about it (a) immediately afterwards, (b) when he saw Mr Wills' reaction? Why did he decide to go to see Mr Wills? If you had been the boy, would you have gone to see Mr Wills?

3 Does what the author tells you about watermelon-stealing in the opening section influence the way you view the boy's behaviour? Do you think the boy behaved badly by stealing the melon and then redeemed himself by going to see Mr Wills? What is your view of the morality of the boy's behaviour?

4 a) Talk about the parts played in the story by the boy's friends — Freddy Gray and J.D. — and by Willadean Wills.

b) Compare this story with Marjorie Darke's *Truth, Dare or Promise?* What are the 'prizes' in each story? What do you think of that?

5 The story is told in the first person from the boy's point of view. How would it have been different if it had been told from another point of view, e.g. J.D.'s, Willadean's, or Mr Wills', or if it had been told in the third person? Do you think it would have worked as well? Give your reasons.

Role play

So I just had to go and see him
The boy meets Freddy or J.D. and explains what happened when Mr Wills discovered the seed melon had gone, why he decided that he must go and see Mr Wills and what happened when he did.

He shouldn't have done it
Two people who have read the story have an argument about it, because one takes the view that the boy should not have stolen the melon in the first place, while another argues that he was not really doing anything wrong, because it was something everyone expected boys to do, like scrumping apples.

How the author tells the story

1 a) Study the way Mr Wills is presented in the story: (a) in the opening section and up to the point he discovers the theft, (b) when he discovers the theft, (c) in the final scene. Discuss